AA

·GLOVEBOX ATLAS·

TOWN PLANS
OF BRITAIN

Reprinted June 1993
Reprinted March 1993
Reprinted September 1992
1st edition April 1992

Published by The Automobile Association, Fanum House,
Basing View, Basingstoke, Hampshire RG21 2EA

Standard ISBN 0 7495 0495 1
Spiral   ISBN 0 7495 0467 6

Mapping produced by the Cartographic Department of
The Automobile Association.

Printed by BPCC Hazell Books, Paulton and Aylesbury

The contents of this book are believed correct at the time
of printing. Nevertheless, the Publisher can accept no responsibility
for errors or omissions, or for changes in the details
given.

A CIP catalogue record for this book is available from the
British Library.

Map Symbols

AA recommended roads	▬▬▬
Other roads	▬▬▬
Restricted roads	----
Buildings of interest	Museum
Car Parks	P
Parks and open spaces	▭
Churches	†
One way streets	←

CONTENTS

Town plan location map and map symbols
(iii)

Town Plans
2-123

Mileage Chart
124

Town Plans

ABERDEEN

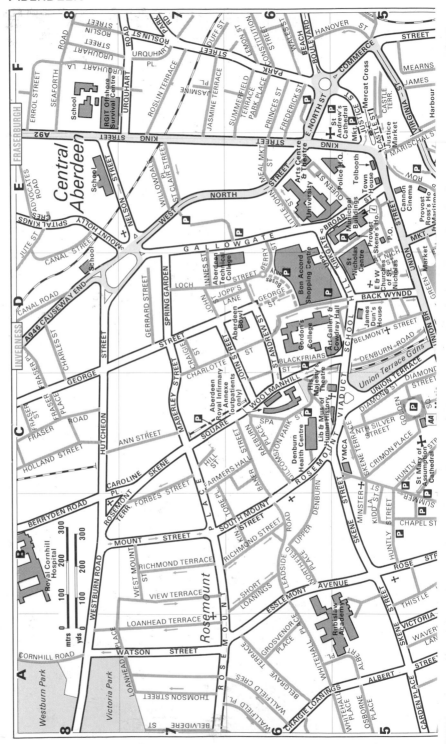

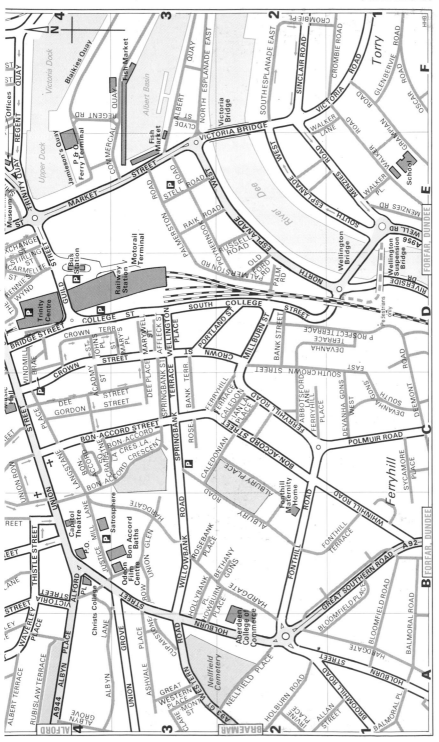

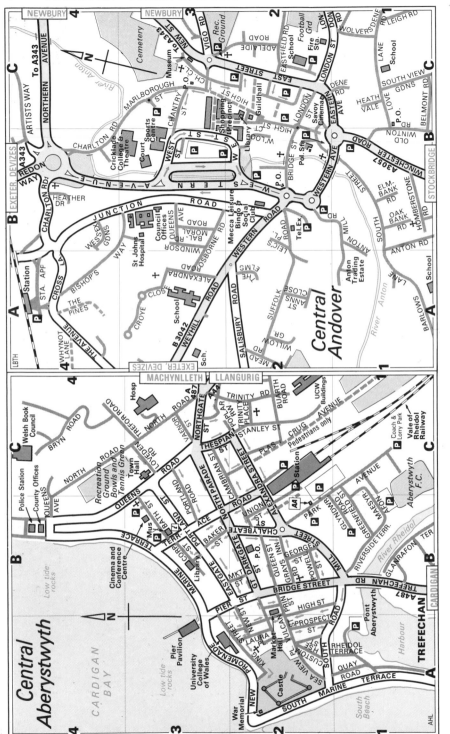

AYR

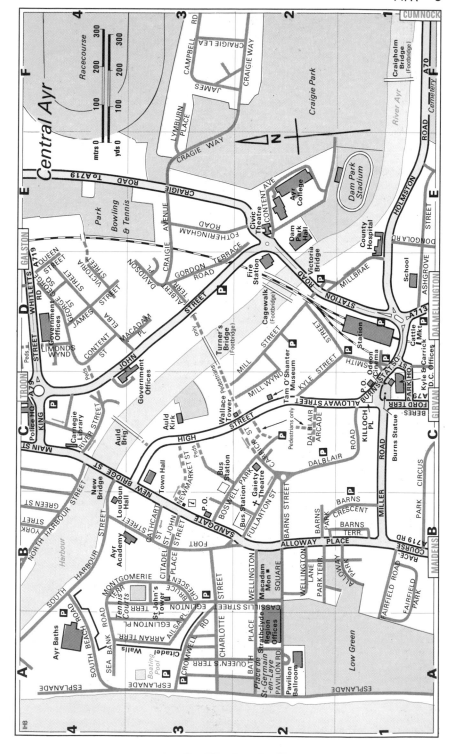

Central Ayr

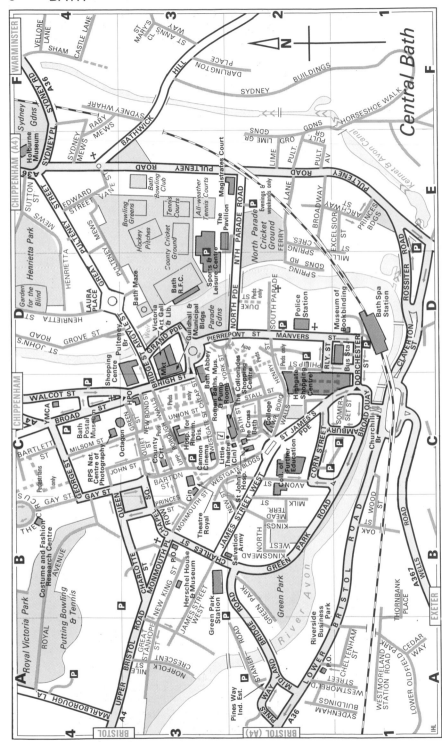

BATH

Central Bath

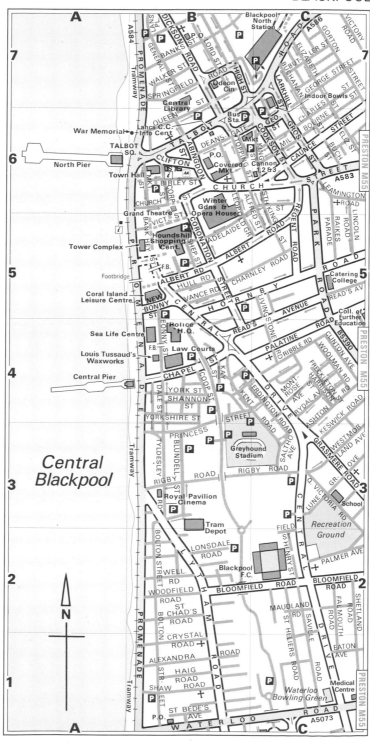

BLACKPOOL

Central
Blackpool

BIRMINGHAM

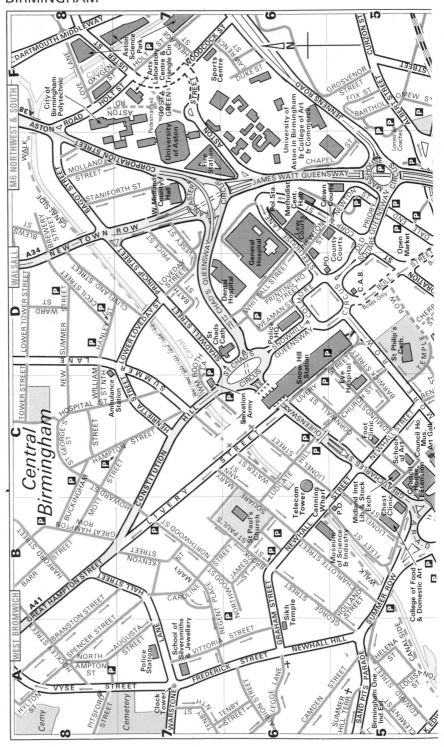

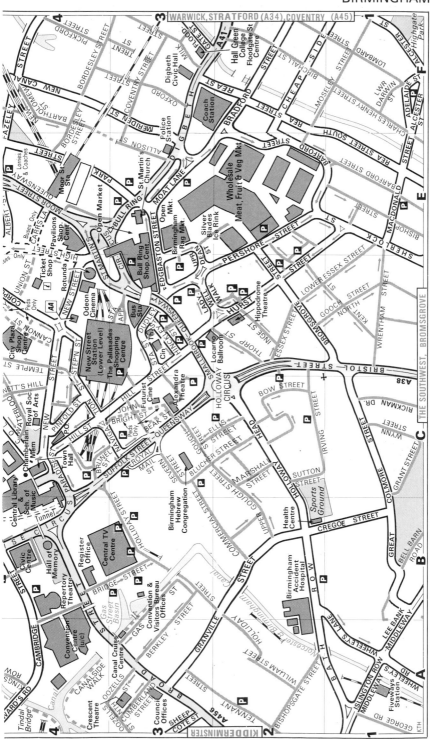

BIRMINGHAM

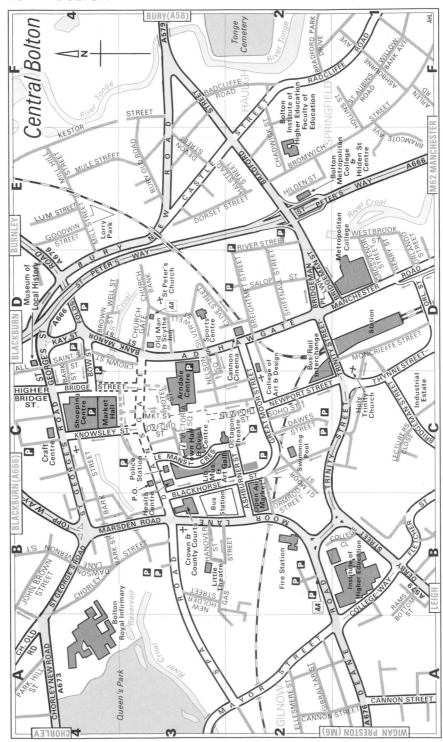

BOLTON

Central Bolton

BOURNEMOUTH

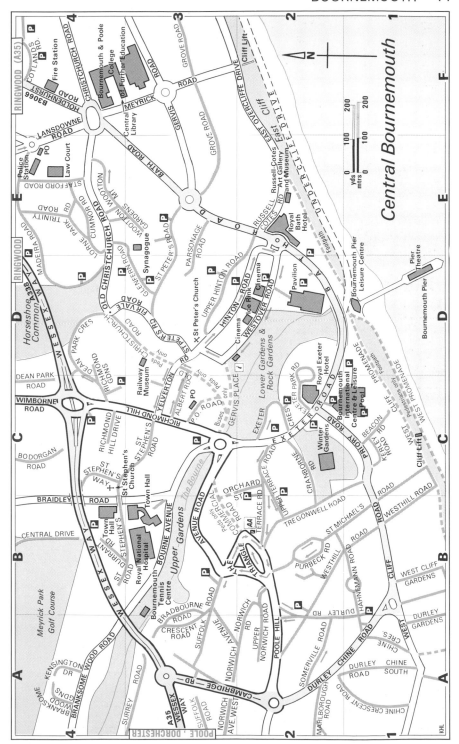

Central Bournemouth

BRISTOL

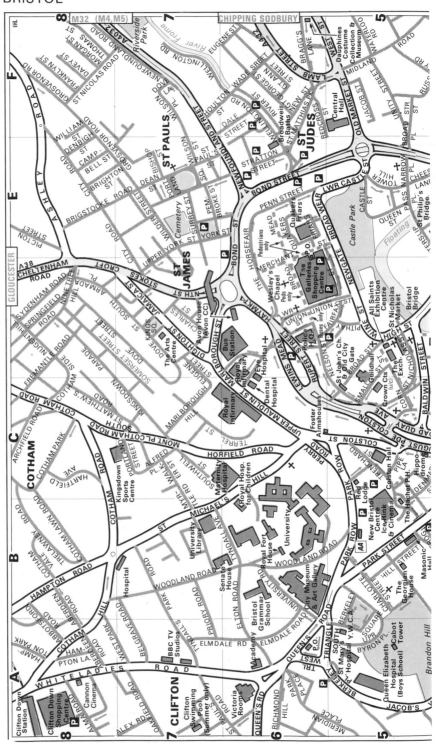

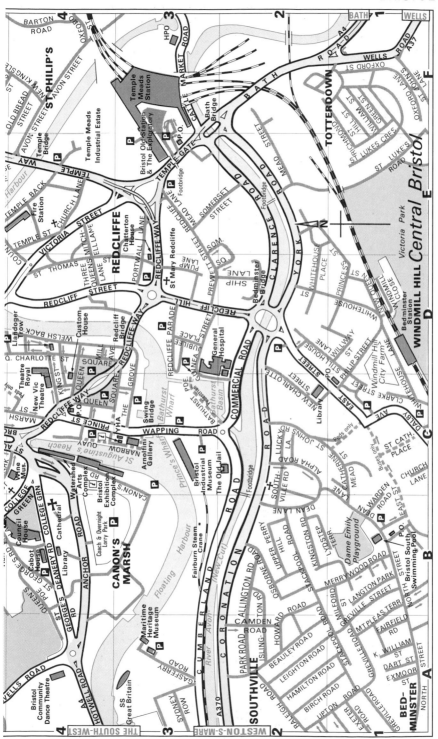

BRADFORD

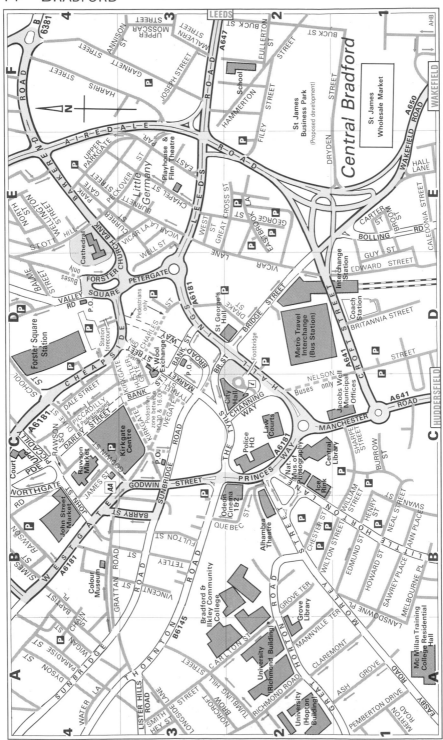

BRIGHTON

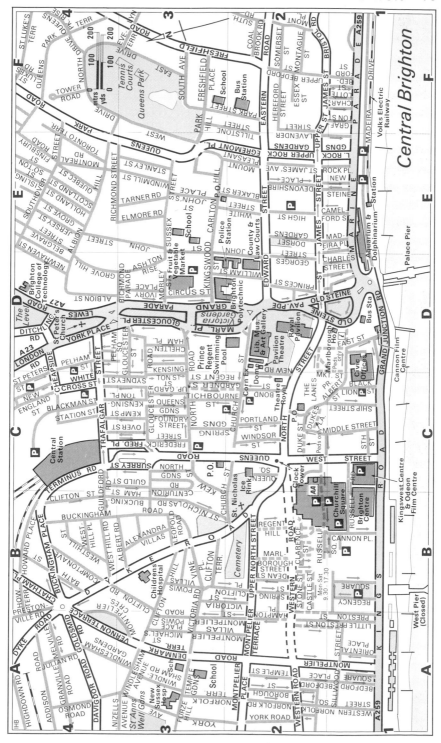

Central Brighton

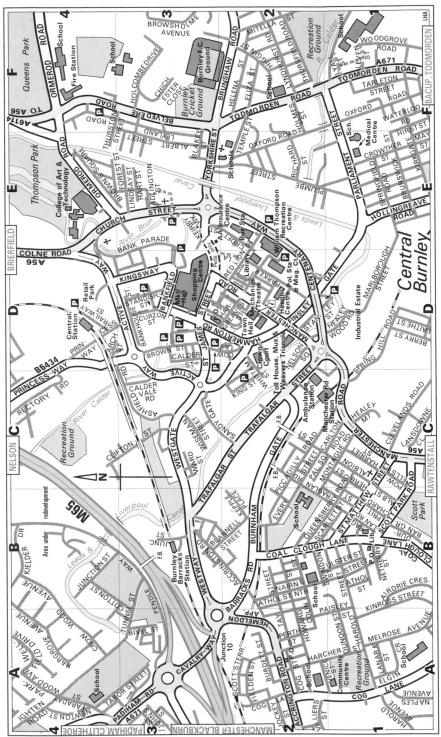

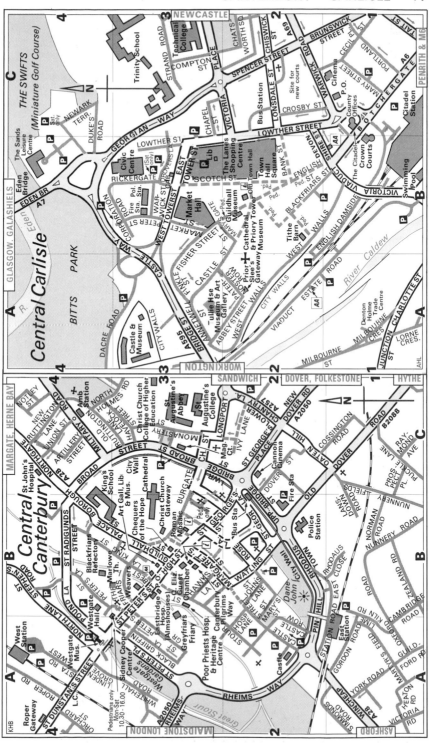

CANTERBURY CARLISLE

CAMBRIDGE

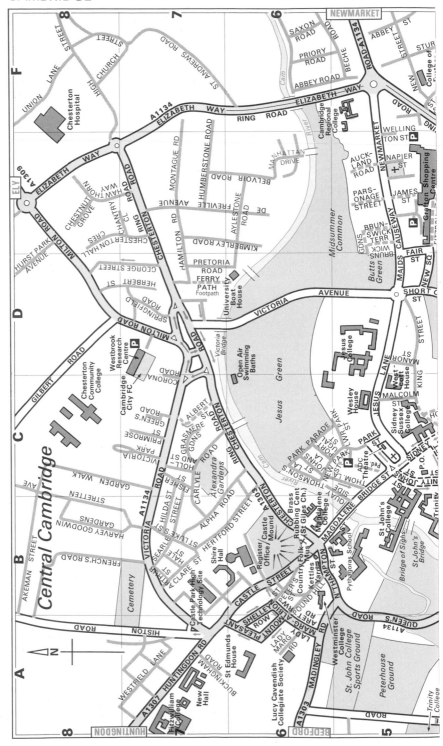

Central Cambridge

CAMBRIDGE

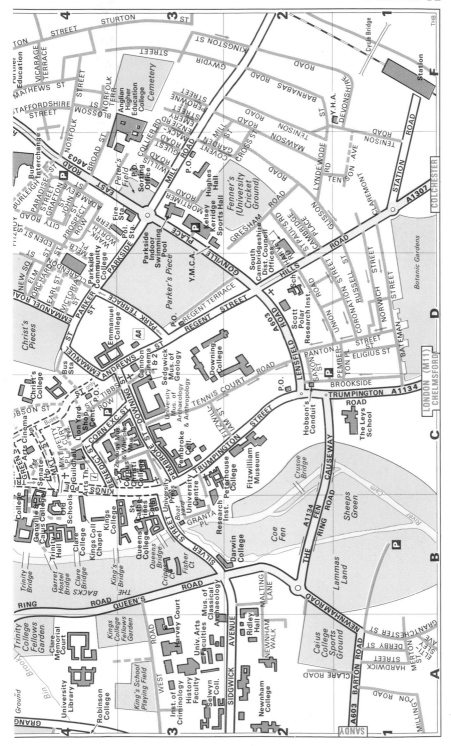

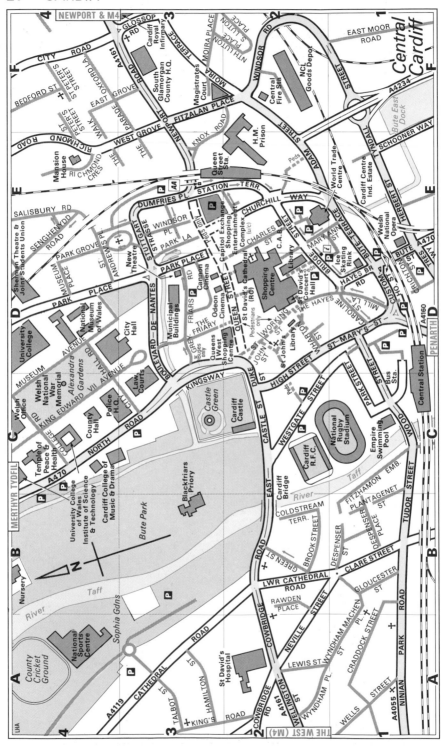

CHESTERFIELD

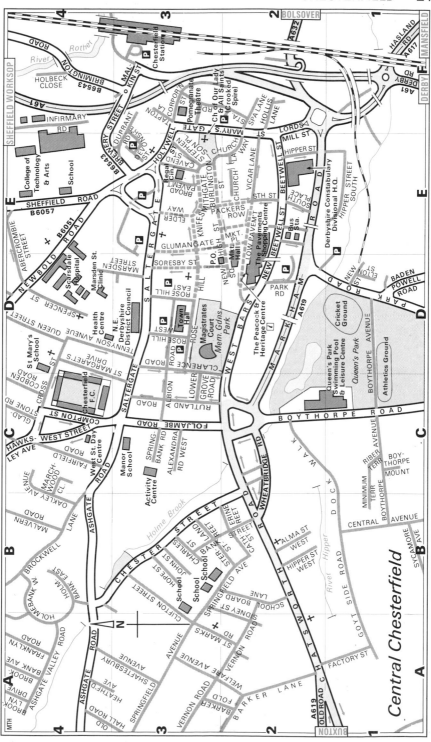

Central Chesterfield

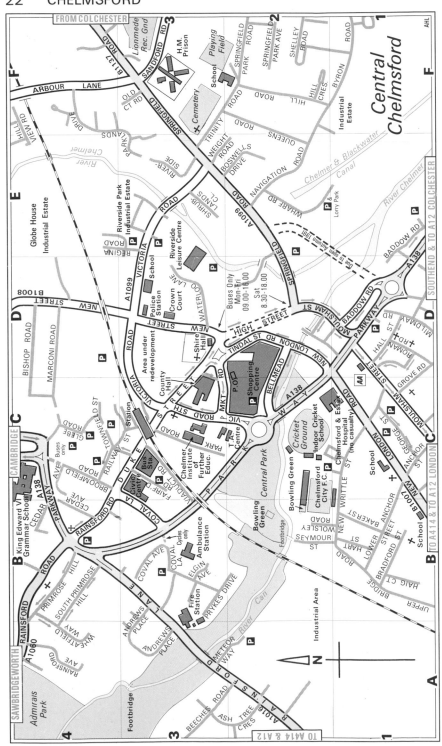

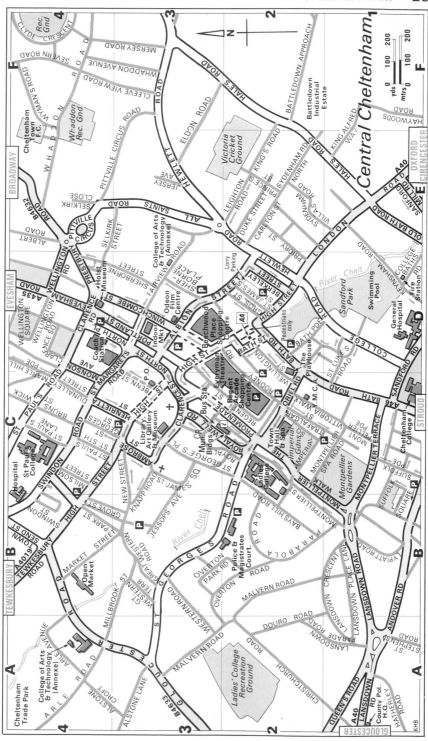

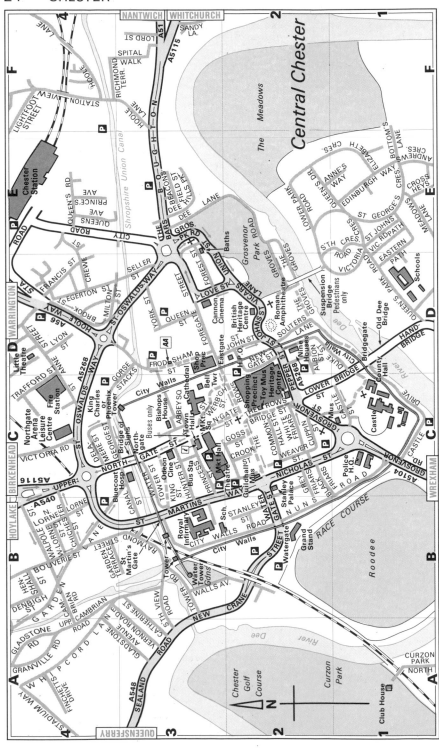

CHESTER

Central Chester

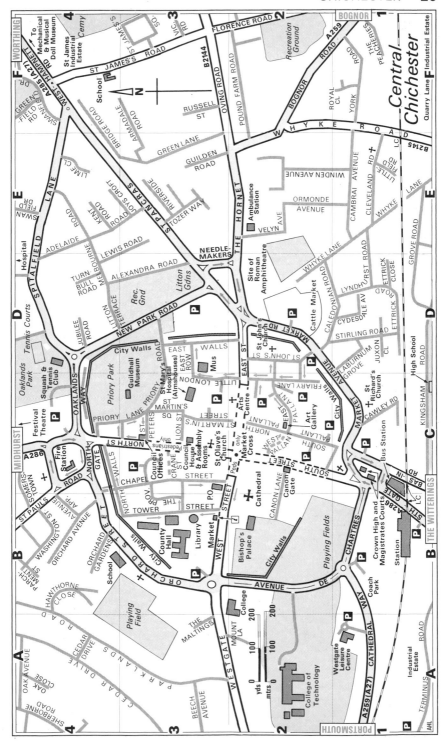

CHICHESTER

Central Chichester

COLCHESTER

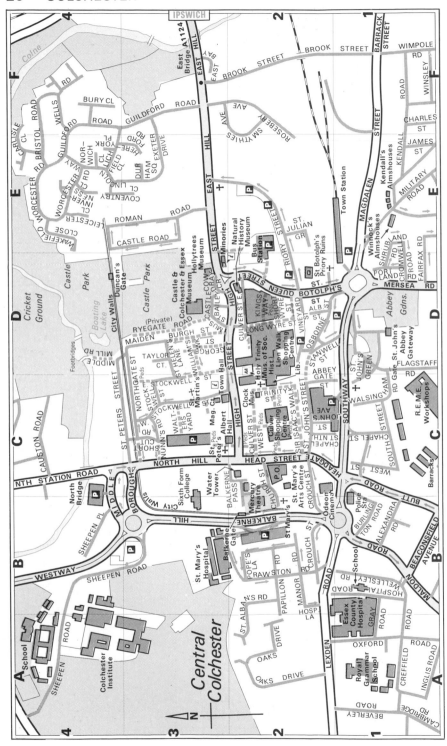

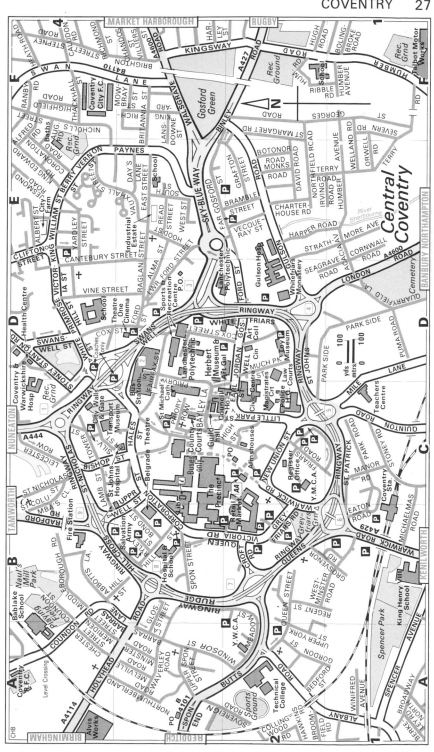

COVENTRY

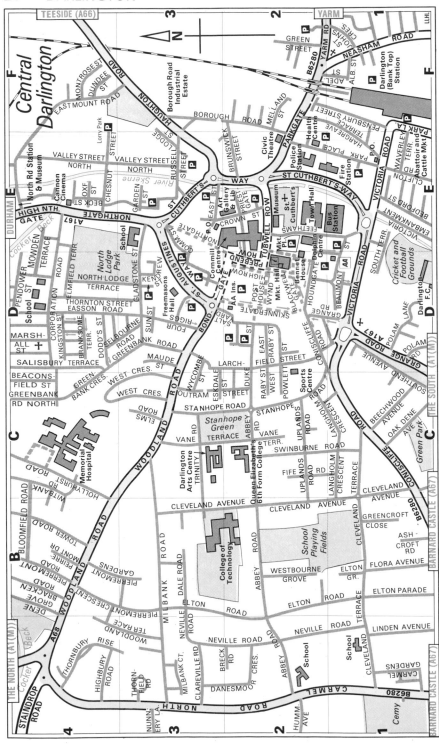

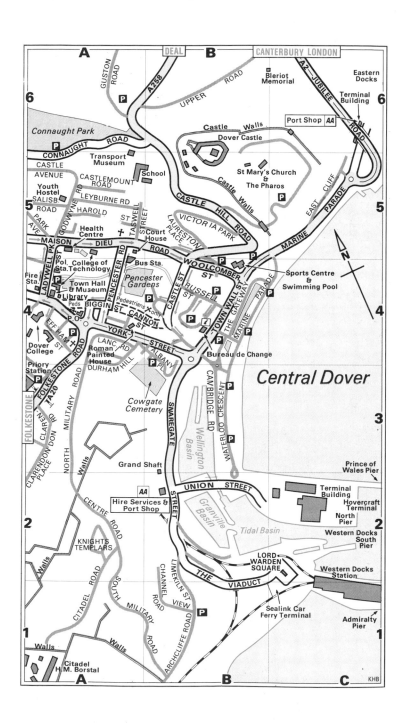

Central Dover

DERBY

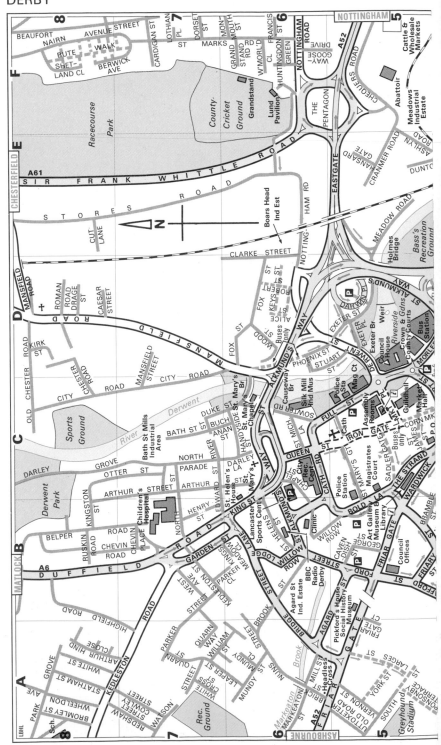

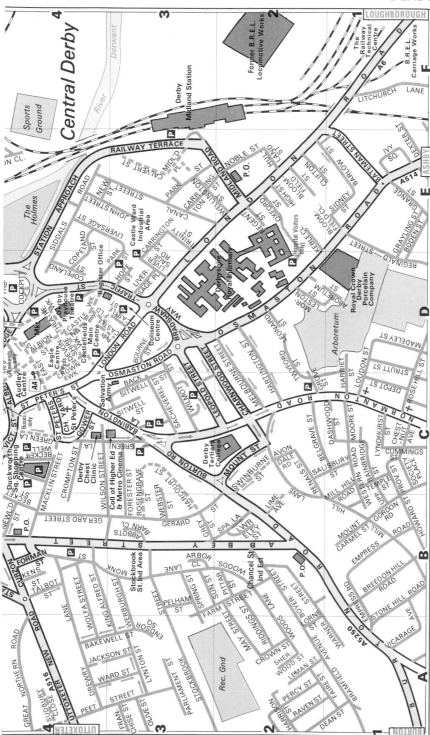

DERBY

Central Derby

DUNDEE

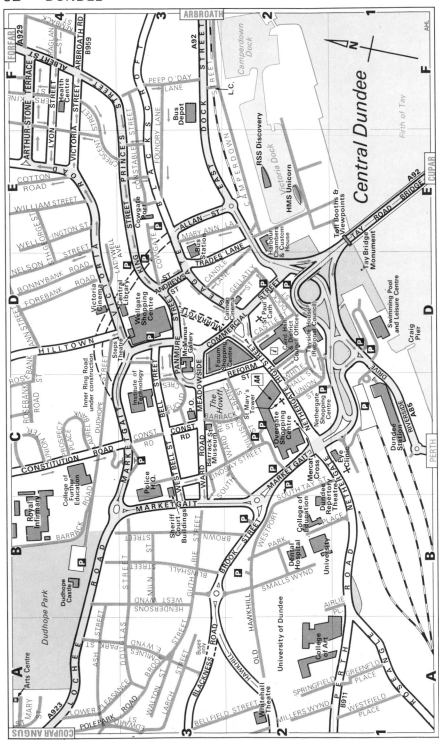

Central Dundee

Firth of Tay

DURHAM

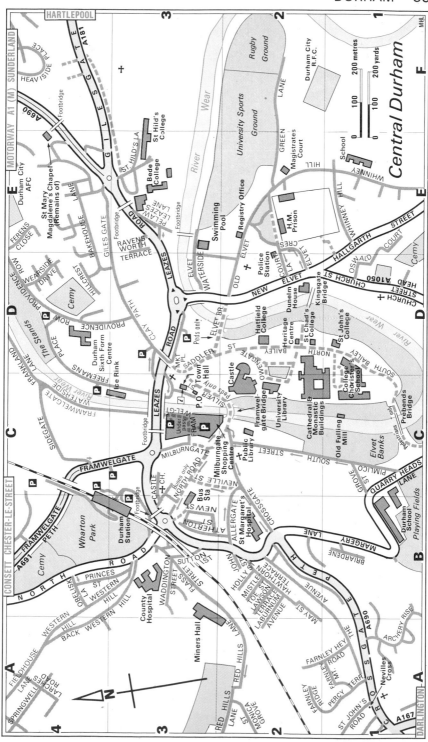

Central Durham

0   100   200 metres
0   100   200 yards

EASTBOURNE

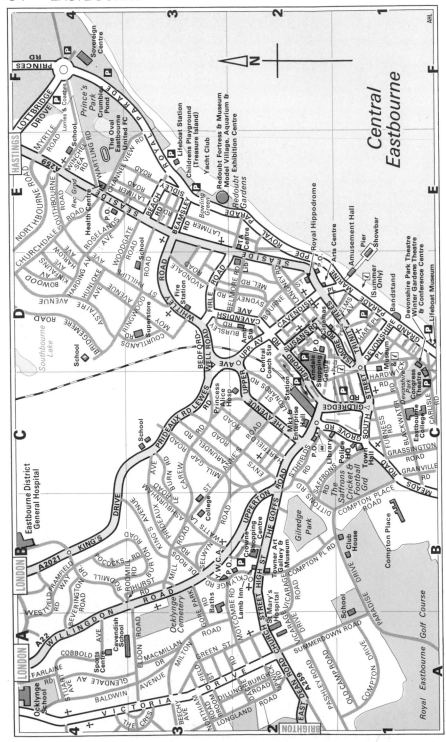

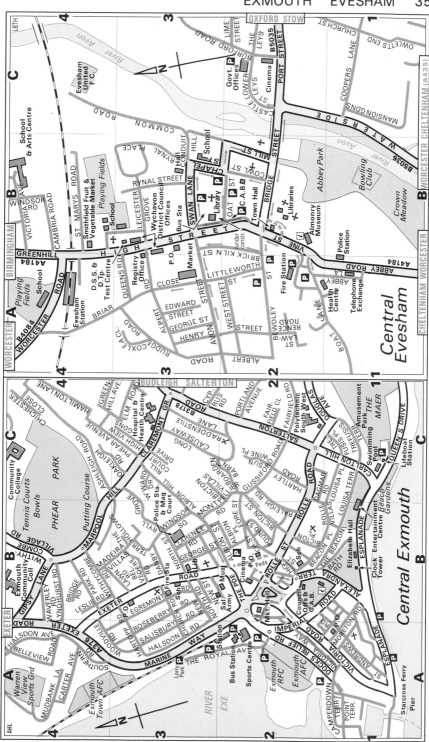

EXMOUTH EVESHAM

Central Evesham

Central Exmouth

EDINBURGH

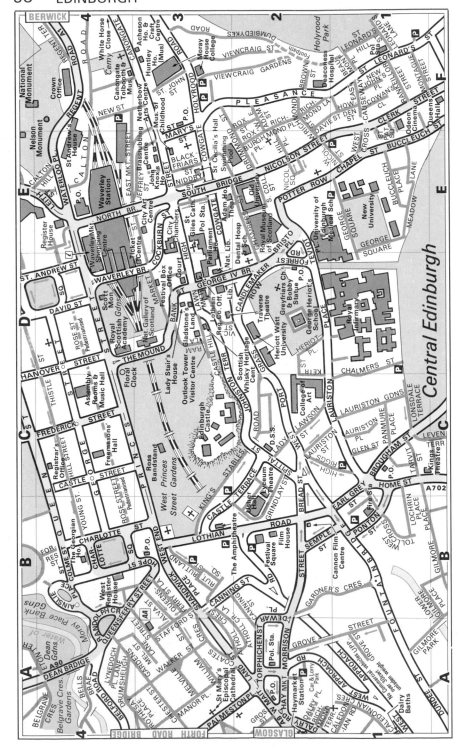

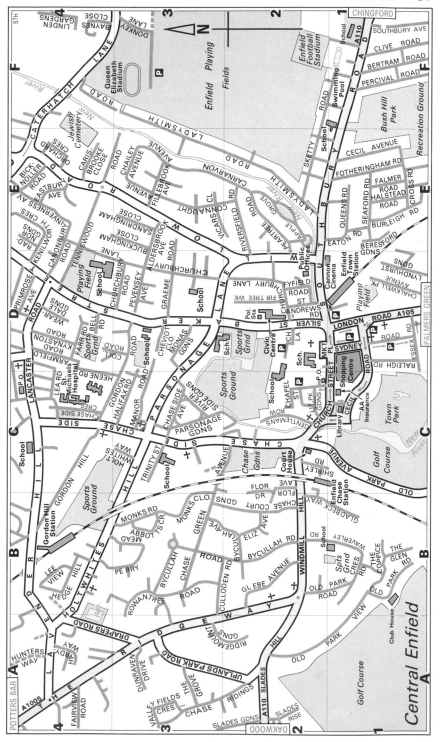

ENFIELD

Central Enfield

EXETER

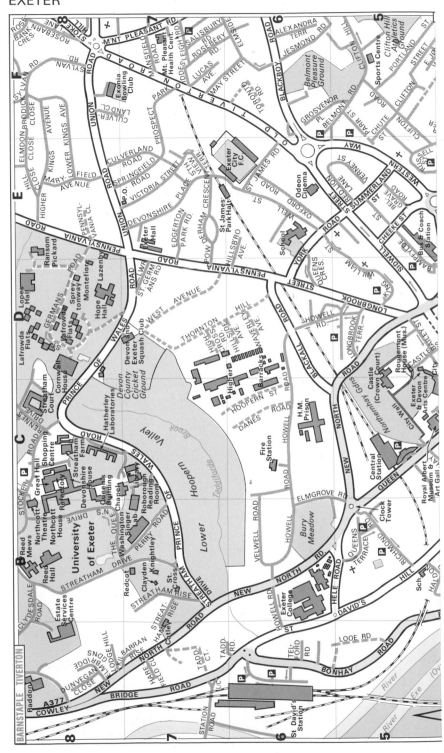

EXETER

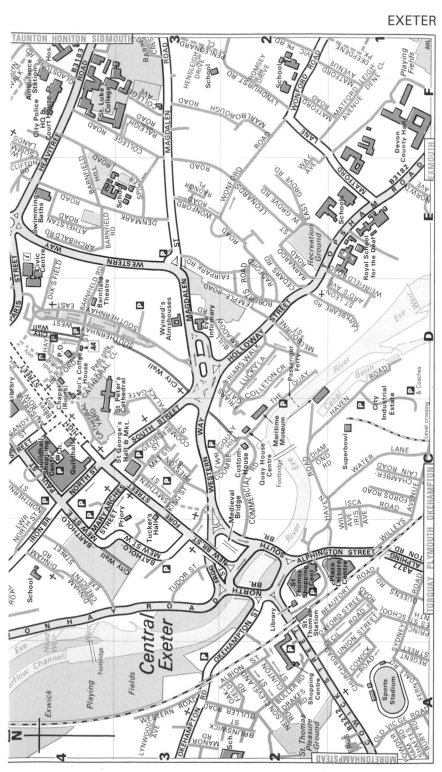

FARNBOROUGH   FELIXSTOWE

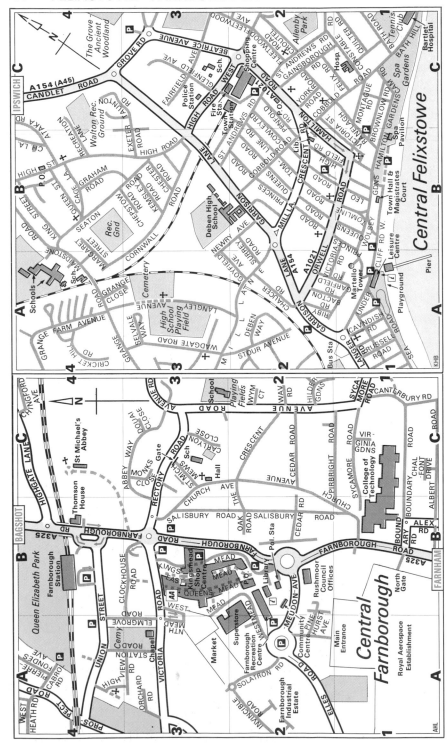

FOLKESTONE

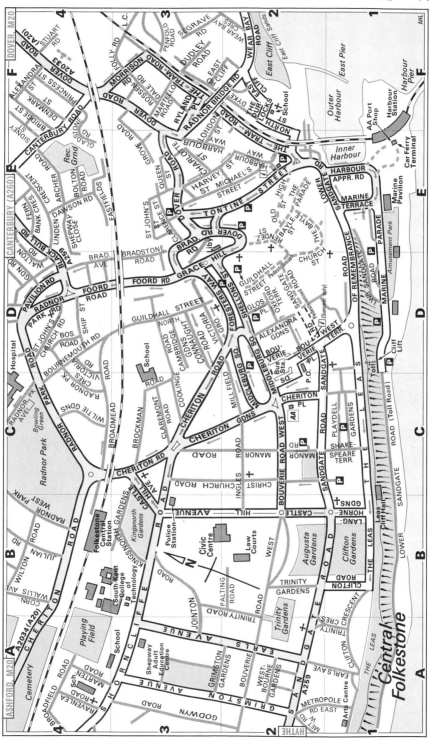

GLASGOW

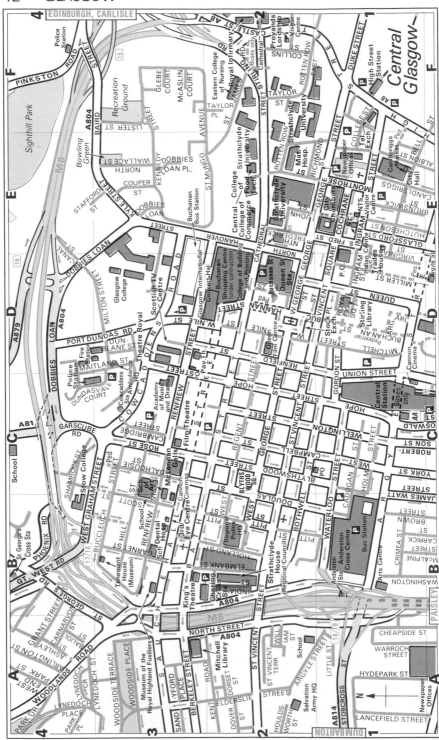

Central Glasgow

Sighthill Park

Police Station
PINKSTON ROAD
STREET
A804
BAIRD ST

Recreation Ground

Bowling Green

Glebe Court
McASLIN COURT

Eastern College of Nursing

Royal Infirmary
Buses only

Provands Lordship
Visitor Centre
COLLINS
Cathedral

High Street Station

Central Glasgow

TAYLOR ST
TAYLOR PL
STREET

ROTTEN ROW
Strathclyde University

DUKE STREET
A8

NORTH WALLACE ST
LISTER ST
KENNEDY STREET
ST MUNGO AVENUE

STAFFORD ST
KYLE STREET
COUPER ST
DOBBIES LOAN PL.
DOBBIES LOAN

Strathclyde University
Strathclyde College of Food Tech
Central College of Commerce

Mat. Hosp.
RICHMOND
Strathclyde University
JOHN
George
City Chambers
COCHRANE
INGRAM

Tel. Exch.
College ST
BELL
ALBION ST
Candleriggs Market
City Hall
CANDLERIGGS
BRUNSWICK ST
HUTCHESON ST

Newspaper Offices

MONTROSE
MILTON STREET
Glasgow College

Buchanan Bus Station
Scottish TV Centre
Theatre Royal
COWCADDENS
DOBBIES LOAN
A804

PORTDUNDAS RD
DUNBLANE ST
MAITLAND ST
Fire Station
Police Station
Sta Ambulance
DUNDASVALE COURT

Buchanan International
Concert Hall
Buchanan Shopping Centre (under contruction)
College of Building and Printing

HANOVER STREET
NTH FREDERICK ST
CATHEDRAL STREET
North Hanover St

Buchanan St
Queen St Sta
W. GEORGE
GEORGE
SQUARE
P.O.

VIRGINIA ST
GLASSFORD ST
INGRAM Outlet Centre Visitor Centre
Trades House
MILLER ST
Argyle St
Ped

QUEEN STREET
W. GEORGE ST
ROYAL EXCH.
Stock Exch.
Stirling Library
Pedestrian
BUCHANAN
MITCHELL ST

Academy of Music and Drama
Film Theatre
McLellan Galls
Sch of Art

RENFREW STREET
W. NILE STREET
NILE STREET
WEST NILE STREET
W. REGENT
RENFIELD STREET
HOPE STREET
WEST CAMPBELL STREET
WEST NILE STREET

Green Film Centre
Pav Th
Ped

ARC
Cannon Cinema

UNION STREET
Central Station
Buses only
A8
OSWALD

ROBERT SON ST

School

A81
GARSCUBE RD
CAMBRIDGE STREET
ROSE ST
SHAMROCK ST
GARNET ST
WEST GRAHAM STREET

STOW COLLEGE
St George's Cross Sta
PHOENIX RD
WEST RD

BUCCLEUCH ST
RENFREW ST
Dental Hosp
3rd Eye Centre Cinemas
Cannon
Sch Art

BLYTHSWOOD SQ
DOUGLAS STREET
GEORGE STREET
WEST REGENT STREET
WEST GEORGE STREET
ST VINCENT STREET
GORDON ST
HOLM ST
CADOGAN ST
WELLINGTON STREET
BOTHWELL STREET

YORK ST
JAMES WATT ST
BROWN ST
CRIMEA ST
CARRICK STREET
McALPINE
WASHINGTON

Anderston Cross Centre
Strathclyde House (Regional Council)
Anderston Sta
Bus Station

Arts Centre

King's Theatre
Tenement House (Museum)
GT WEST RD
GEORGES RD
WOODLANDS RD

GRANT STREET
CARNARVON ST
BALIOL ST
ASHLEY ST
WEST END PK ST

LYNEDOCH PLACE
WOODSIDE TERRACE
WOODSIDE PLACE

Museum of the Royal Highland Fusiliers

BERKELEY STREET
SAND-Y-FORD
KENT RD
ELDERSLIE ST
DOVER ST
DORSET ST
ELMBANK ST
HOLLAND ST
PITT STREET
WATERLOO STREET
DOUGLAS STREET

Mitchell Library
A804
NORTH STREET
ST VINCENT STREET
ST VINCENT TERR
WILLIAM ST
School
Salvation Army HQ

HOULDS-WORTH ST
ARGYLE STREET
LITTLE STREET
STOBCROSS ST
A814

CHEAPSIDE ST
WARROCH STREET
HYDEPARK ST
LANCEFIELD STREET
Newspaper Offices

PAISLEY
DUMBARTON

GUILDFORD

Central Guildford

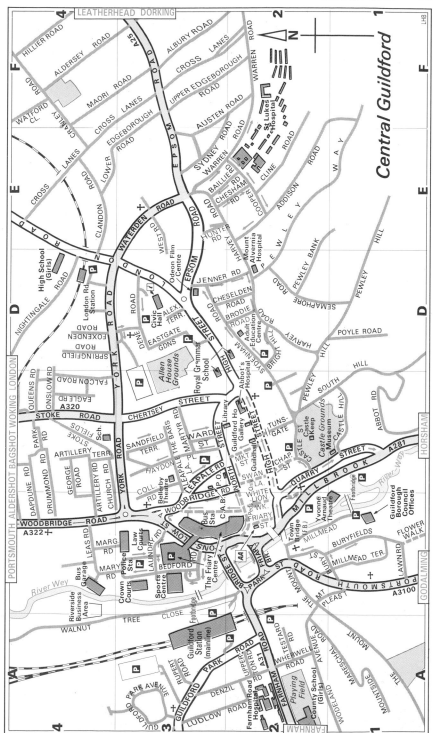

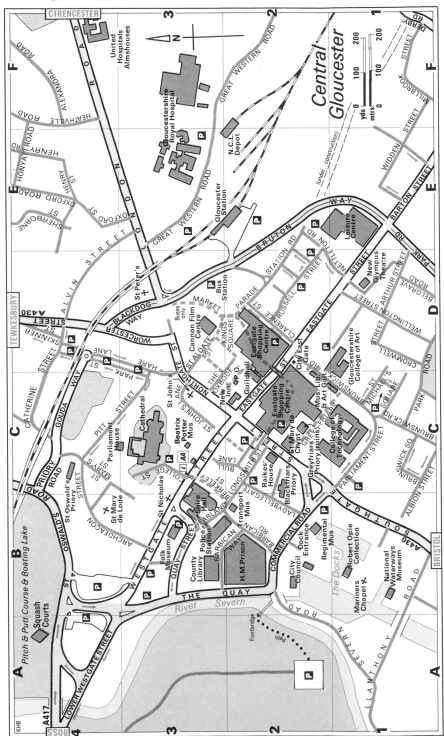

GLOUCESTER

Central Gloucester

United Hospitals Almshouses

Gloucestershire Royal Hospital

N.C.L. Depot

Gloucester Station

St Peter's

Bus Station

Leisure Centre

New Olympus Theatre

Cannon Film Centre

Kings Square

Market

Eastgate Shopping Centre

City East Gate

Gloucestershire College of Art

Guildhall

New Inn

Eastgate Shopping Centre

Mus. Lib. & Art Gall.

Cathedral

St John's

Beatrix Potter Mus

St Mary de Crypt

Greyfriars Priory (ruins)

College of Technology

Parliament House

Raikes' House

Blackfriars Priory

St Mary de Lode

St Oswald's Priory

St Nicholas

Shire Hall

Police Station

Folk Museum

County Library

H.M. Prison

Transport Mus

Barbican

City Council

Regimental Mus

Robert Opie Collection

National Waterways Museum

Mariners Chapel

The Docks

Dock Entrance

Footbridge

River Severn

THE QUAY

Squash Courts

Pitch & Putt Course & Boating Lake

CIRENCESTER

TEWKESBURY A430

ROSS

A417

BRISTOL A430

DERBY RD

BARTON STREET

GREAT WESTERN ROAD

BRUTON WAY

EASTGATE STREET

BLACKDOG WAY

WORCESTER STREET

NORTHGATE STREET

SOUTHGATE STREET

WESTGATE STREET

THE QUAY

COMMERCIAL ROAD

LLANTHONY ROAD

SEVERN ROAD

PRIORY ROAD

GOUDA WAY

ALVIN STREET

LONDON ROAD

SKINNER STREET

ALEXANDRA ROAD

HEATHVILLE ROAD

HENRY ROAD

HONYATT ROAD

OXFORD ROAD

SHERBORNE ST

HENRY ST

STATION RD

NETTLETON RD

RUSSELL STREET

CLARENCE ST

PARADE

BELGRAVE ROAD

PARK RD

WELLINGTON STREET

BRUNSWICK RD

WIDDEN STREET

MILLBROOK STREET

CROMWELL STREET

BRUNSWICK SQ

ALBION STREET

PARK STREET

ST MICHAEL'S SQUARE

ST JOHN'S LANE

ST ALDATE ST

HARE LANE

PARK ST

PITT ST

ST MARY'S ST

COLLEGE ST

ARCHDEACON ST

LONGSMITH ST

BERKELEY ST

BULL LANE

LADYBELLEGATE ST

BARBICAN WAY

LOWER WESTGATE STREET

ST OSWALD'S ROAD

CATHERINE STREET

KHB

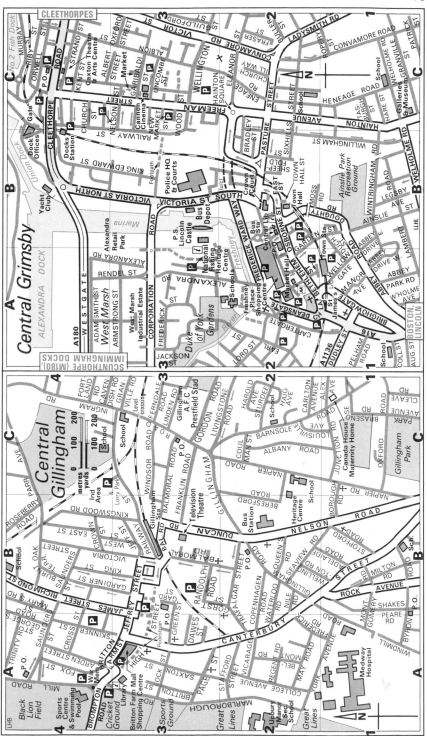

GILLINGHAM   GRIMSBY

Central Grimsby

Central Gillingham

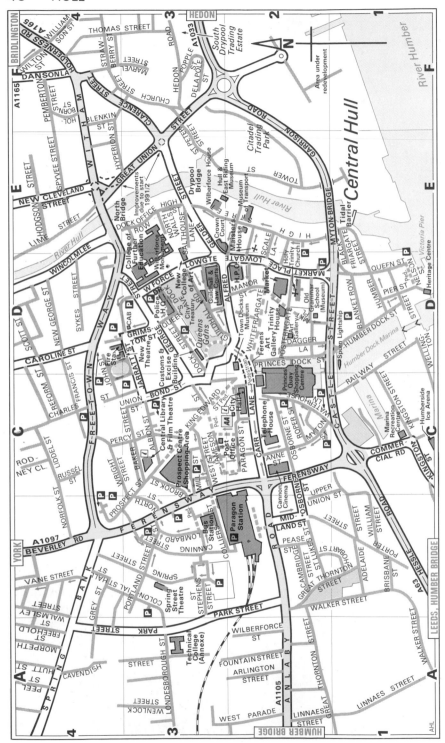

HULL

BRIDLINGTON A165

HEDON

South Drypool Trading Estate

Area under redevelopment

River Humber

N

Central Hull

River Hull

THOMAS STREET

WILLIAM SON ST

WILTON ST

HORNESS RD

DANSONLA

A1165

PEMBERTON STREET

NEW GEORGE ST

NEW CLEVELAND STREET

LHODGSON ST

LIME STREET

River Hull

WINCOLMLEE

SCOTT ST

CAROLINE ST

CREFORM ST

CHARLES ST

ROD- NEY CL.

NORFOLK ST

LIDDEL ST

RUSSEL ST

FREE-TO-WN WAY

WRIGHT STREET

PROSPECT ST

BAKER ST

NORTH

Fire Stn.

JARRATT ST

JOHN ST

ALBION ST

PERCY ST

College of Further Education

North Bridge

DOCK OFFICE

Wilberforce Monument

Wilberforce House

Hull & East Riding Museum

Crown Court

Mandela Gardens

Holy Trinity Church

Old Grammar School (Museum)

Guildhall & Law Courts

City Treasury

College of Art

New College

Town Docks Museum

Ferens Art Gallery

Trinity House

DAGGER LA

Spurn Lightship

Humber Dock Marina

Marina

Victoria Pier

Heritage Centre

QUEEN ST

PIER ST

NELSON ST

HUMBER ST

BLANKET ROW

HUMBER DOCK ST

WELLINGTON STREET

KINGSTON STREET

Marina Recreation Centre

Humberside Ice Arena

COMMER- CIAL RD

Princes Quay Shopping Centre

Telephone House

City Hall

Post Office

Central Library & Film Theatre

Prospect Centre Shopping Area

Cannon Cinema

FERENSWAY

Paragon Station

Bus Station

COLLIERS

Spring Street Theatre

PARK STREET

Technical College (Annexe)

WILBERFORCE ST

FOUNTAIN STREET

ARLINGTON STREET

WEST PARADE

LINNAEUS STREET

GREAT THORNTON STREET

WALKER STREET

A63 HESSLE

LEEDS, HUMBER BRIDGE

YORK A1097 BEVERLEY RD

SPRING BANK

VANE STREET

WALMSLEY ST

FREEHOLD ST

MORPETH ST

HUTT ST

PEEL ST

CAVENDISH

WENLOCK STREET

LONDESBOROUGH ST

PORTLAND STREET

COLON ST

GREY ST

A1105

ANLABY

A1097

HUMBER BRIDGE

AHL

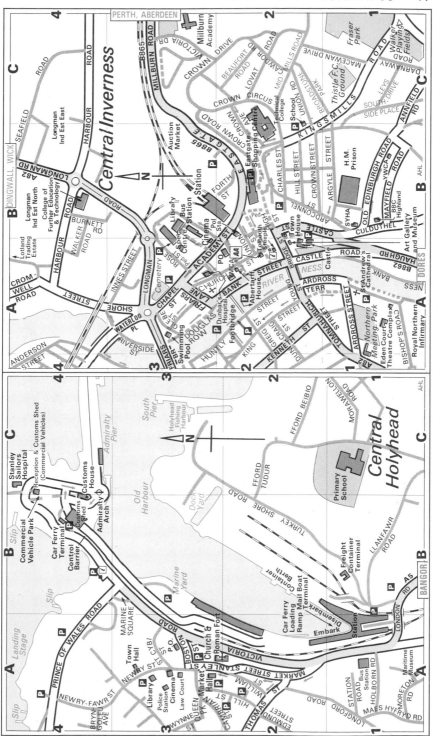

HOLYHEAD   INVERNESS

IPSWICH

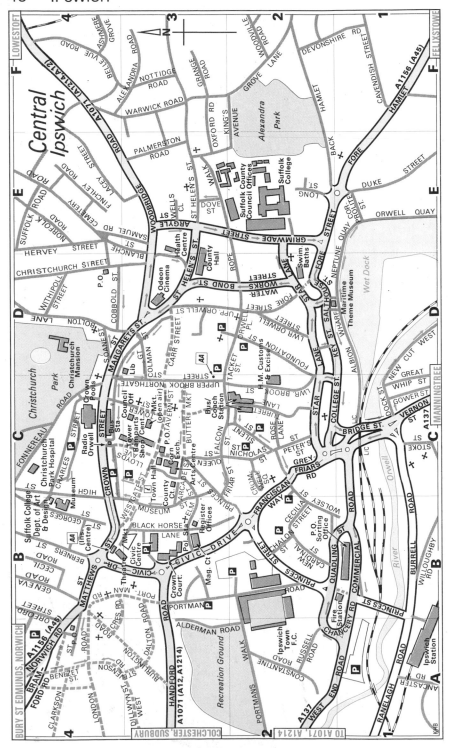

Central Ipswich

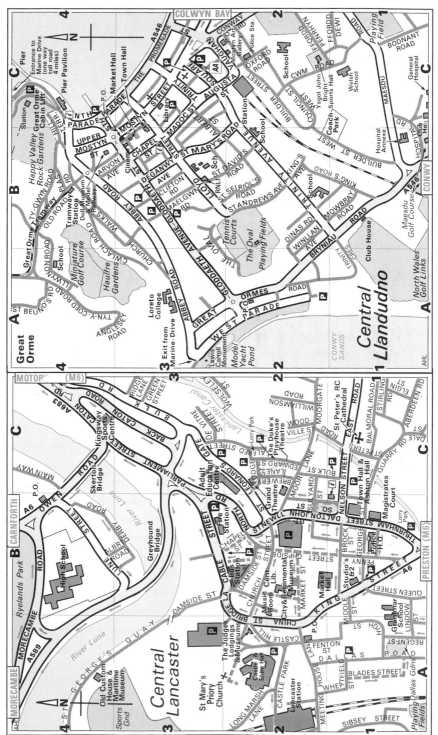

LLANDUDNO

LANCASTER

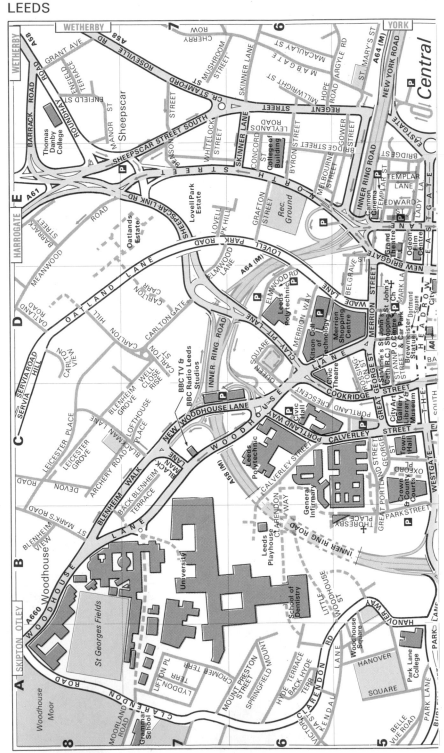

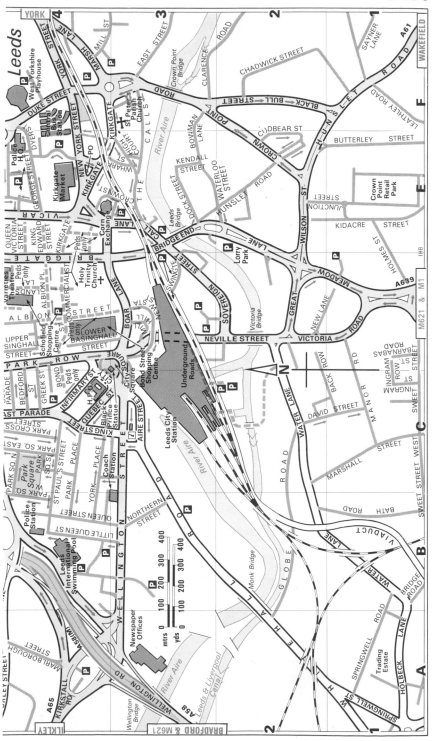

Leeds

LEICESTER

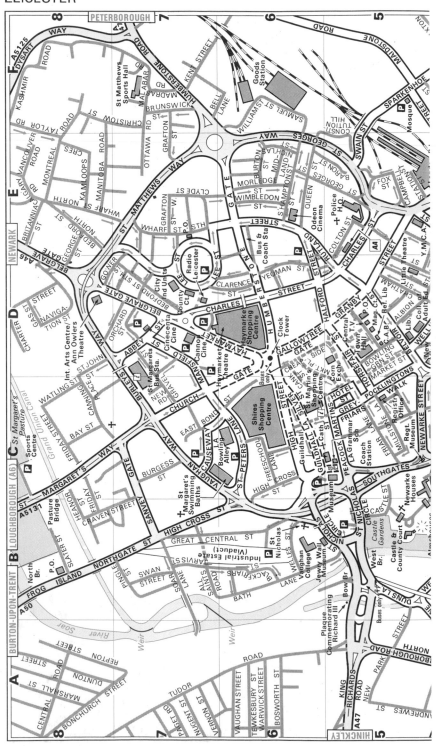

LEICESTER

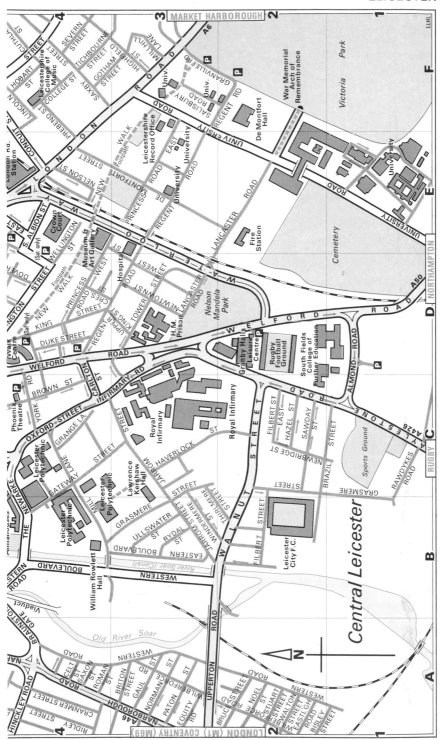

Central Leicester

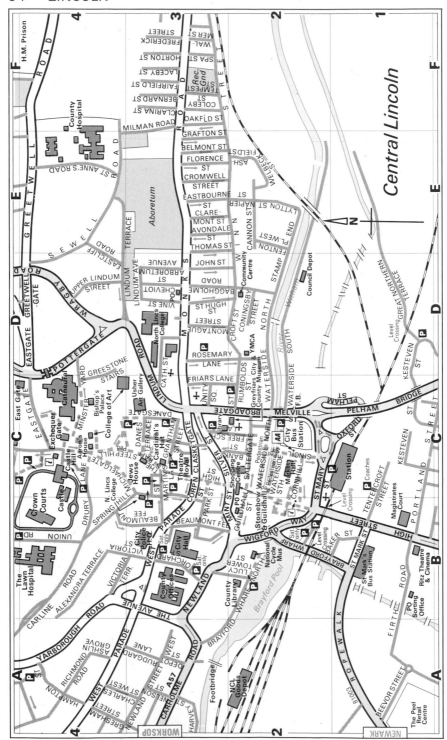

LINCOLN

Central Lincoln

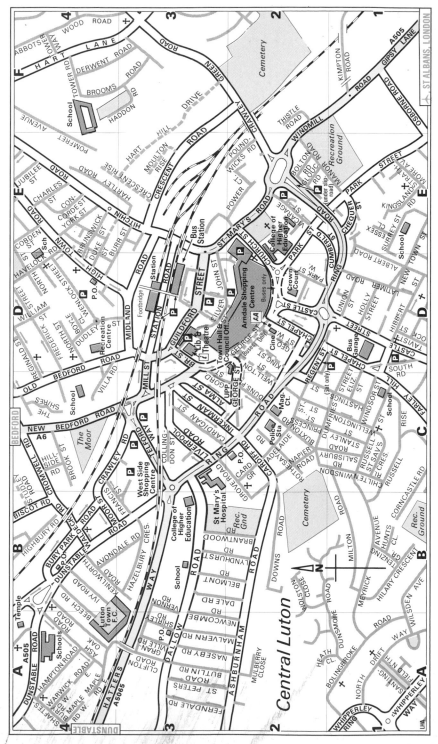

LUTON

Central Luton

LIVERPOOL

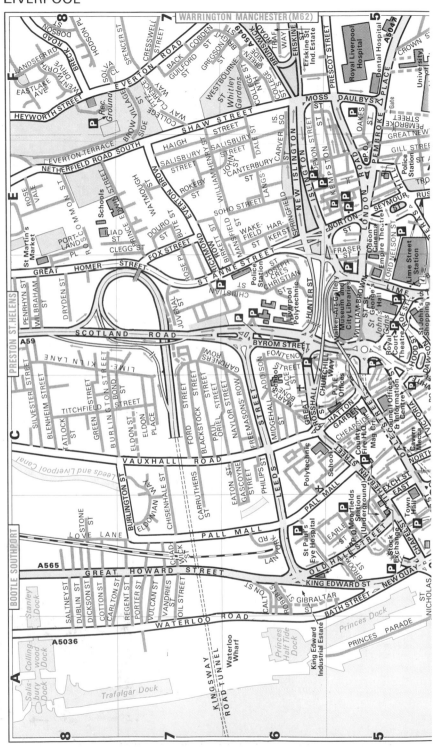

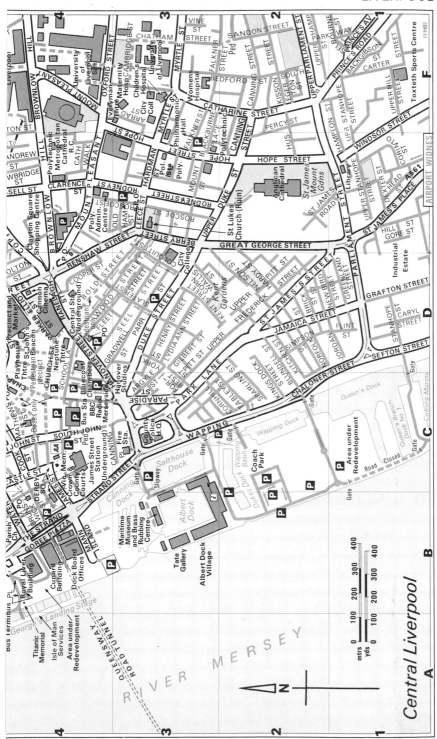

LIVERPOOL

Central Liverpool

RIVER MERSEY

AIRPORT WIDNES (11/HB)

N

LONDON

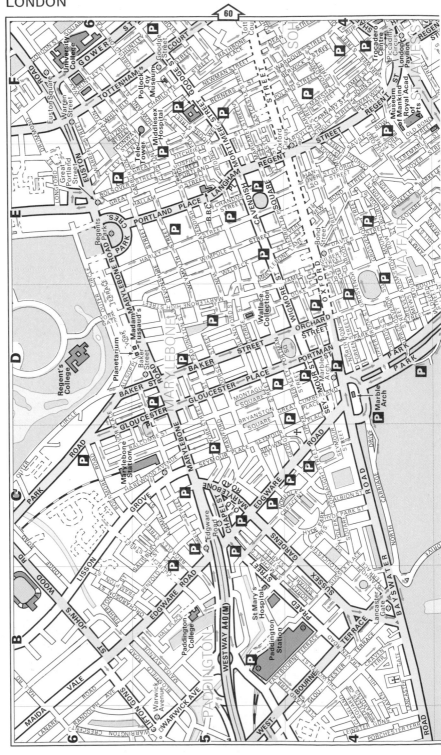

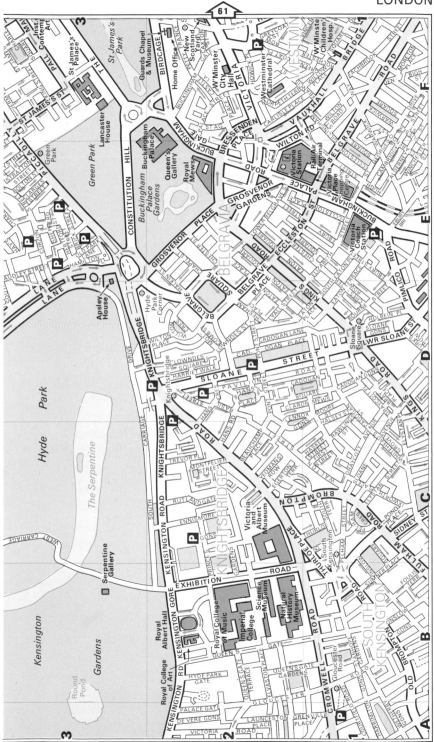

LONDON

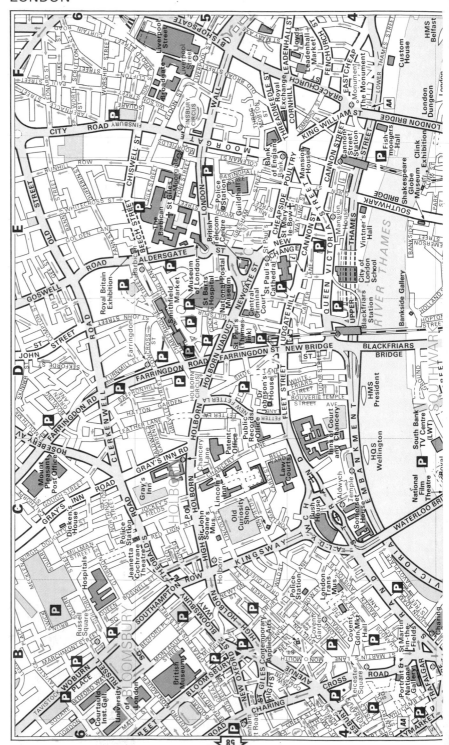

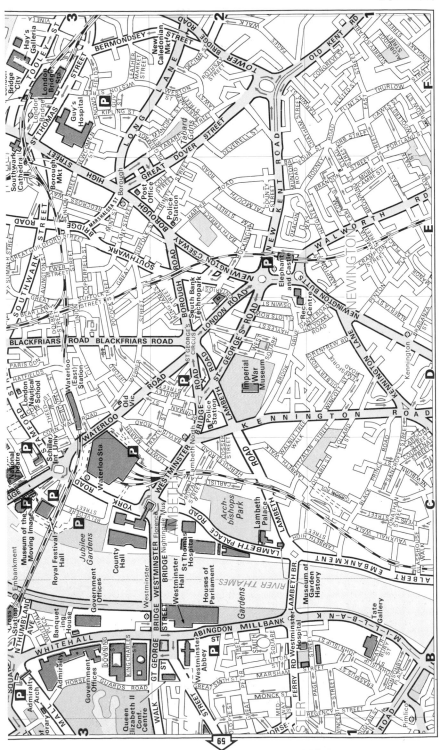

LONDON

MANCHESTER

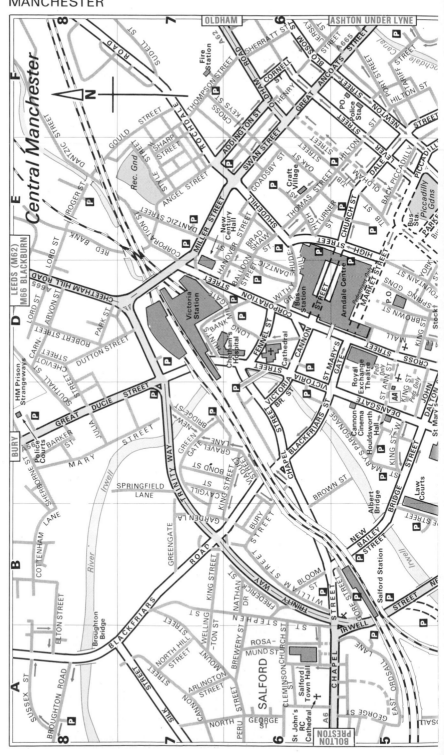

Central Manchester

MANCHESTER

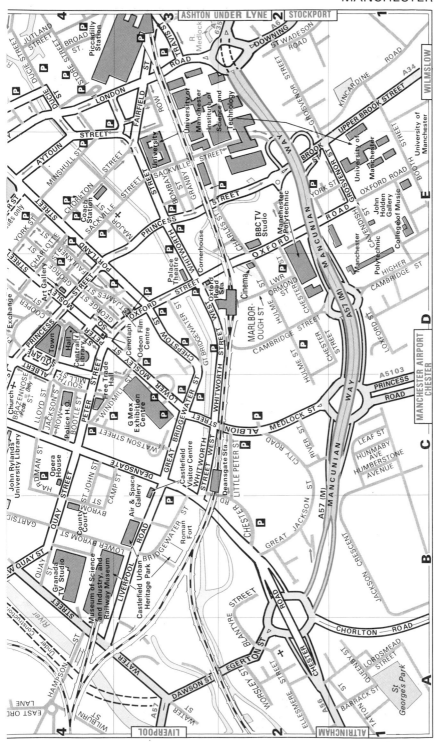

MAIDENHEAD MAIDSTONE

MAIDSTONE

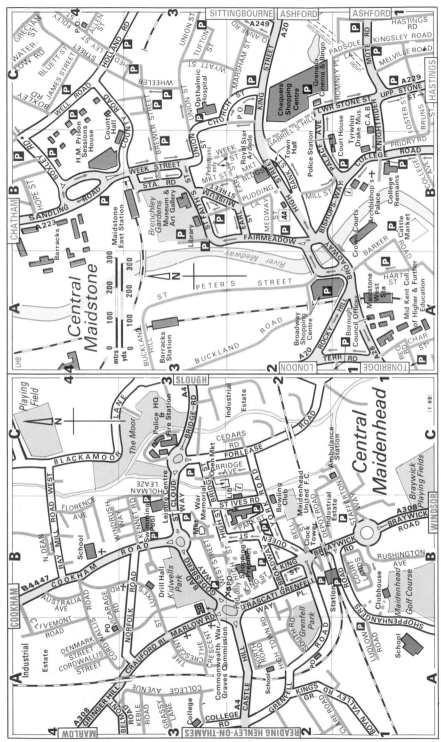

Central Maidstone

Central Maidenhead

MIDDLESBROUGH

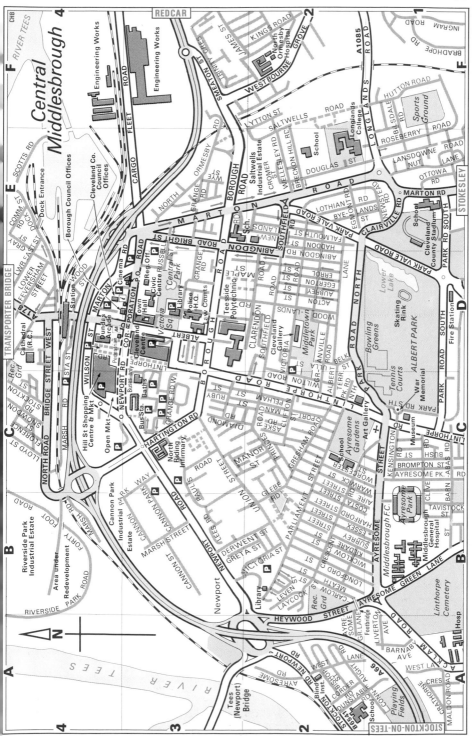

MILTON KEYNES

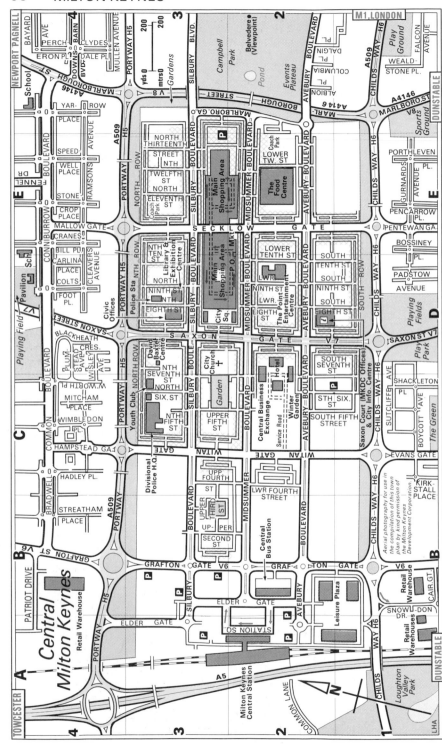

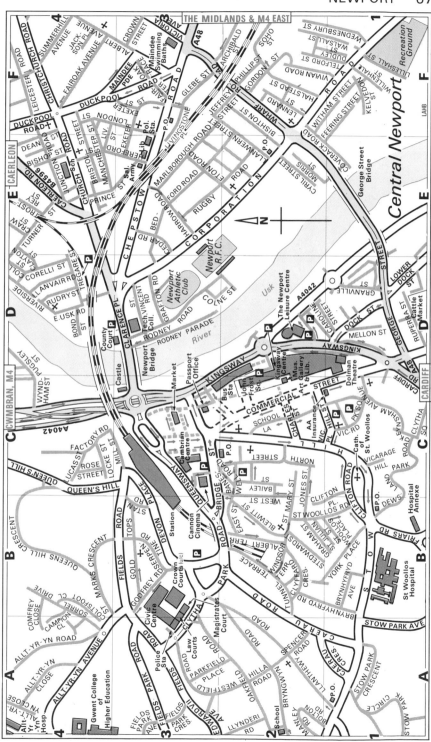

NEWCASTLE UPON TYNE

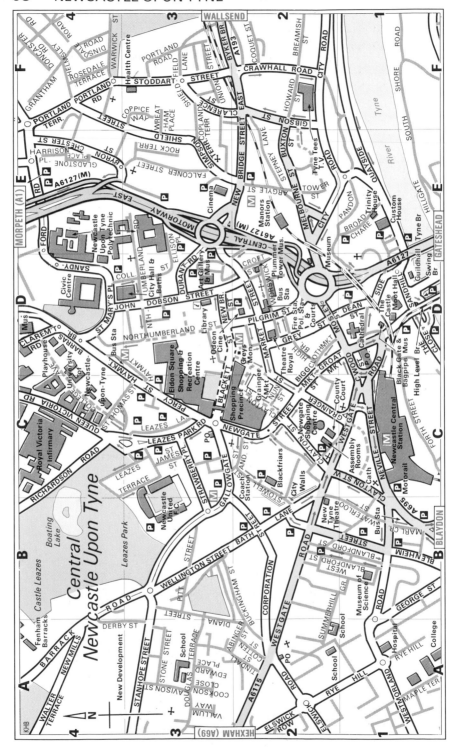

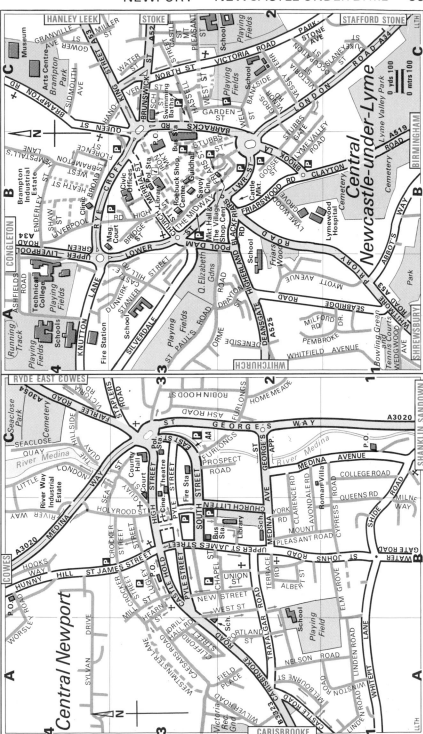

NEWPORT   NEWCASTLE UNDER LYME

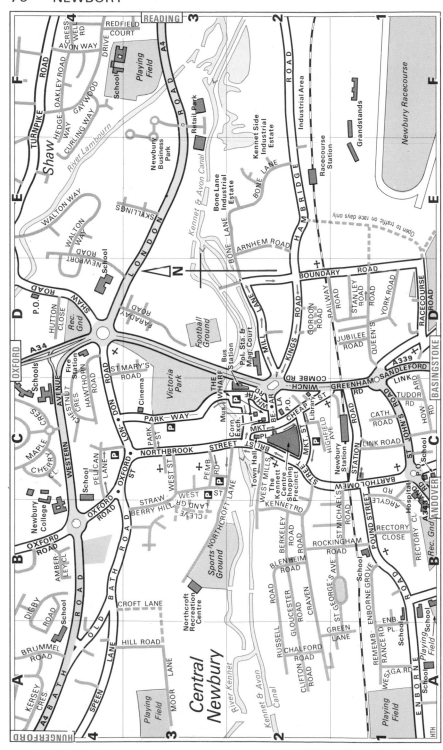

NEWBURY

Newbury Racecourse

Grandstands

Racecourse Station

Industrial Area

Kennet Side Industrial Estate

BONE LANE

Bone Lane Industrial Estate

Open to traffic on race days only

HAMBRIDGE ROAD

Boundary ROAD

RAILWAY ROAD
STANLEY ROAD
YORK ROAD
GORDON ROAD
KINGS ROAD
JUBILEE ROAD
QUEEN'S
A339
SANDLEFORD LINK
RACECOURSE ROAD
TUDOR RD
HOW RD
CATH. ROAD
LINK ROAD
ST JOHN'S ROAD

BASINGSTOKE

ARNHEM ROAD

MILL LANE

Pol. Sta. & Mag. Court
Bus Station

WINCH
GREENHAM RD
COMBE RD

Library
P.O.
HIGHFIELD AVE
MKT. ST.
Newbury Station

CHEAP ST
BRIST
MKT PL.
The Kennet Centre Shopping Precinct
Town Hall

BARTHOLOMEW
ST. School
P.O.
ARGYLE RD
A343
ANDOVER
School
Hospital
RECTORY CL.
RECTORY CLOSE

REMEMB. RANCE PL.
ENB. PL.
School
Playing Field
School
WEST
G.A. RD.
ENBORNE
Playing Field

REDFIELD COURT
Playing Field
CRESS WELL RD
AVON WAY
DRIVE
A4
REDFIELD COURT
School

READING

TURNPIKE ROAD
HEDGE WAY
OAKLEY ROAD
CURLING WAY
GAYWOOD

Shaw

River Lambourn

Retail Park
Newbury Business Park

WALTON WAY
SKILLINGS
WALTON WAY
NEWPORT ROAD
School
LONDON ROAD
SHAW ROAD

Kennet & Avon Canal

FARADAY ROAD
Football Ground

HUTTON CLOSE
P.O.
Rec. Gnd

OXFORD
A34

Fire Station
ST MARY'S ROAD
HAWTHORN ROAD
Cinema
Victoria Park

Schools
AVENUE
CHESTNUT CRES
CHERRY CL.
MAPLE CRES

WESTERN AVENUE

PELICAN LANE
School
Newbury College
OXFORD ROAD
LON-DON ST

AMBER LEY CL
BATH ROAD

PARK ST
PARK WAY
NORTHBROOK STREET
WEST ST
STRAW BERRY HILL
CLEVE LAND GR
NORTHCROFT LANE
PEMB RD
WEST ST

THE WHARF
WHARF RD
Mus.
BE-AR
P
P
Corn Exch.
P
P

West Mills
KENNET RD
BERKELEY ROAD
BLENHEIM ROAD
RUSSELL ROAD
GLOUCESTER ROAD
CHALFORD ROAD
CLIFTON ROAD
CRAVEN ROAD
GREEN LANE
ST GEORGE'S AVE
ROCKINGHAM ROAD
ST MICHAEL'S ROAD
POUND STREET
ENBORNE GROVE

Sports Ground
Northcroft Recreation Centre

DIGBY ROAD
School
BRUMMEL ROAD
KERSEY CRES
A4 BATH ROAD
OLD BATH ROAD
SPEEN LANE
CROFT LANE
HILL ROAD
MOOR LANE
Playing Field

Central Newbury

River Kennet
Kennet & Avon Canal

HUNGERFORD

Rec. Gnd

N

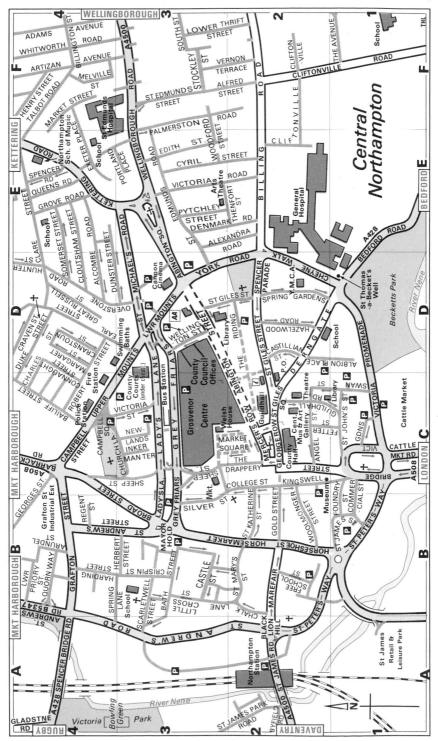

NORTHAMPTON

NORWICH

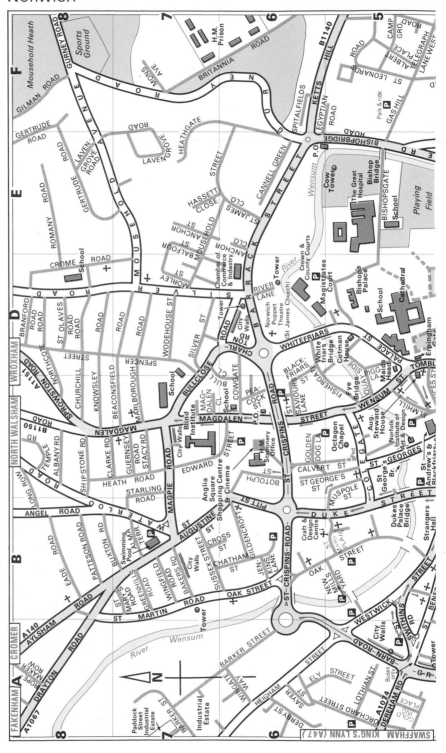

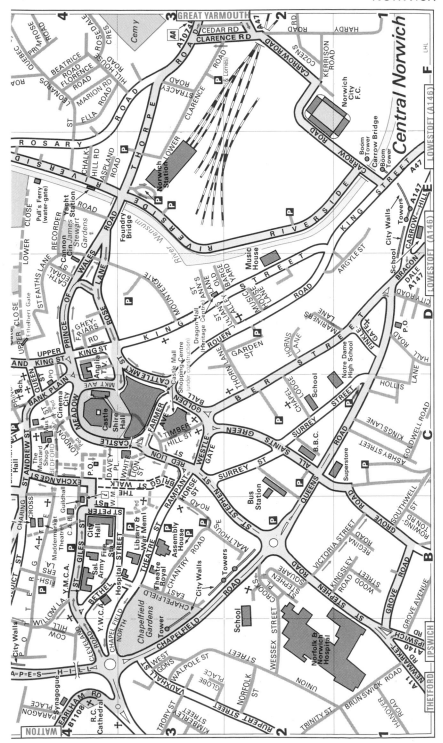

Central Norwich

NOTTINGHAM

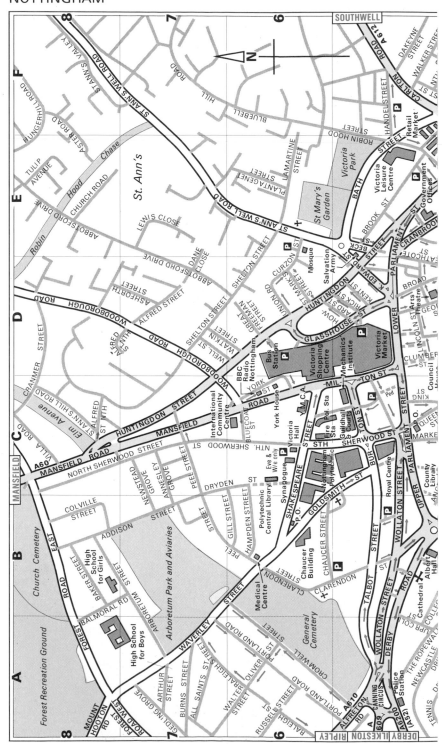

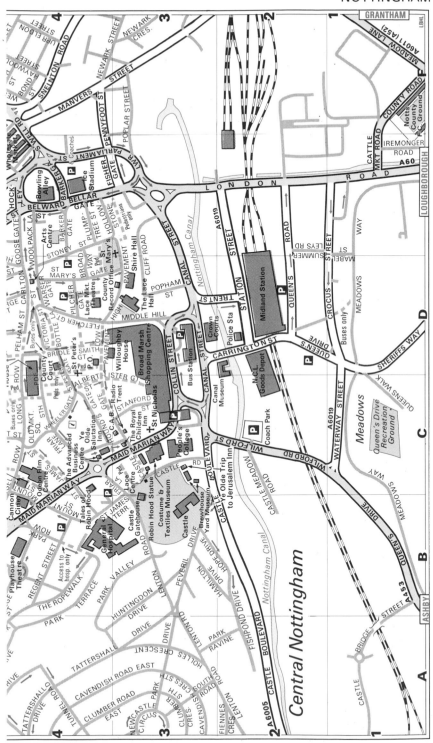

OXFORD

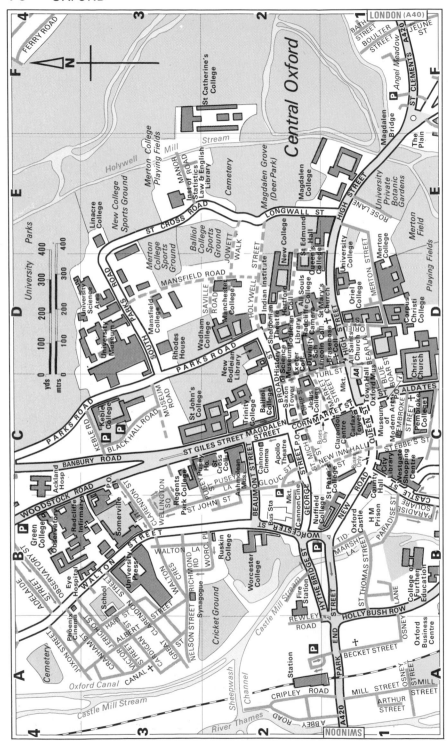

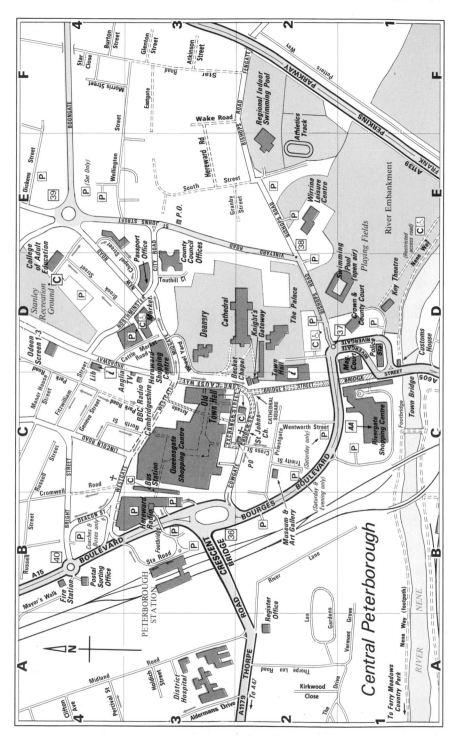

PETERBOROUGH

Central Peterborough

PLYMOUTH

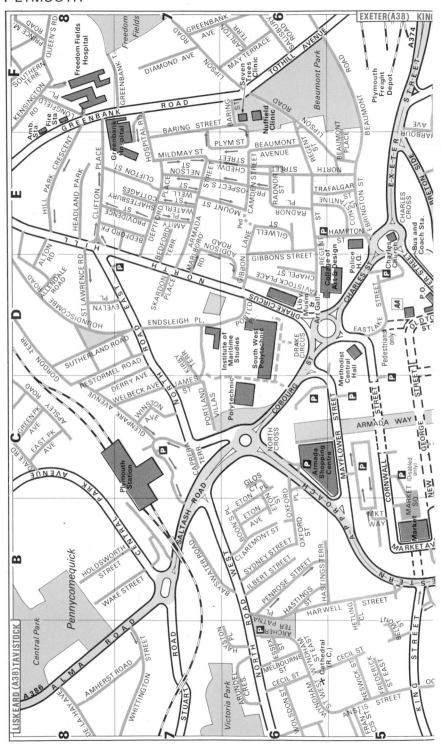

PLYMOUTH

Central Plymouth

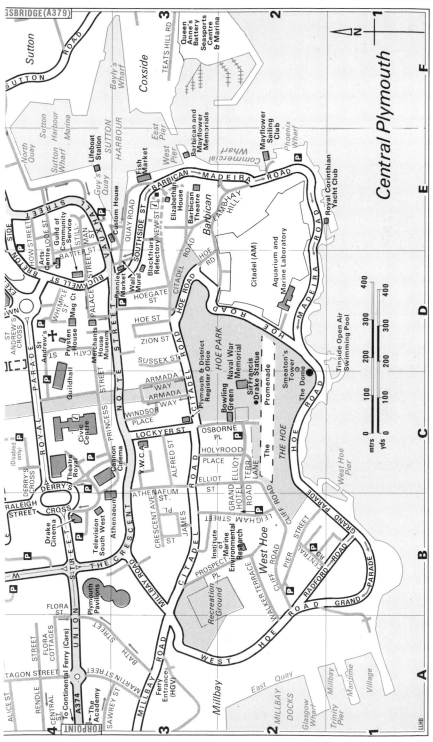

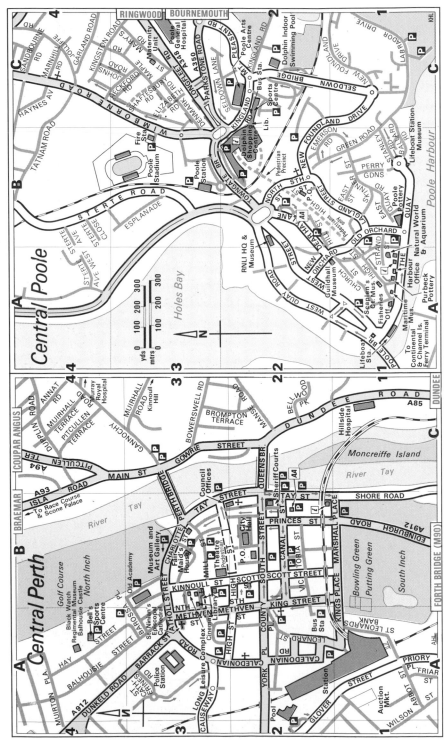

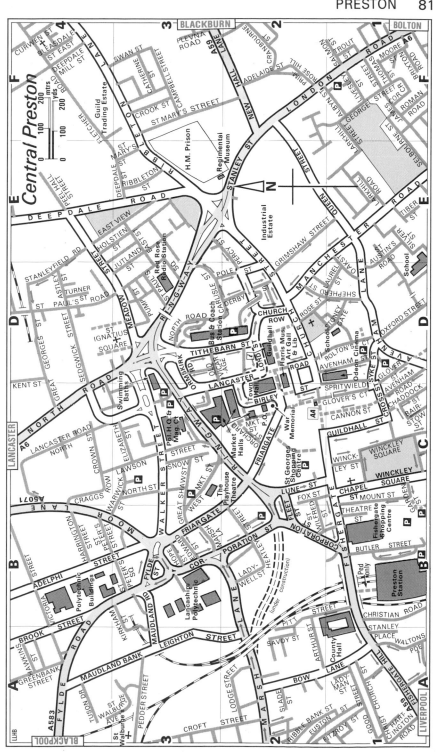

PRESTON

Central Preston

PORTSMOUTH

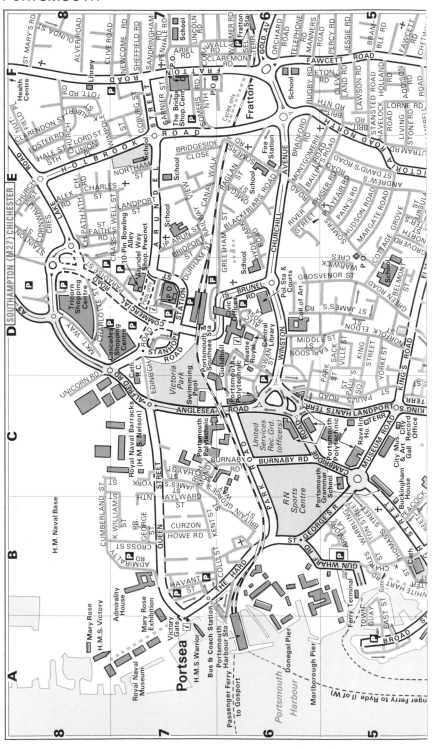

PORTSMOUTH

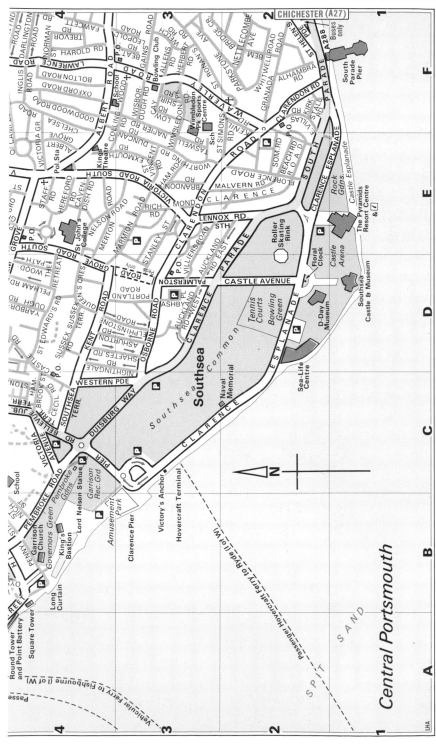

Central Portsmouth

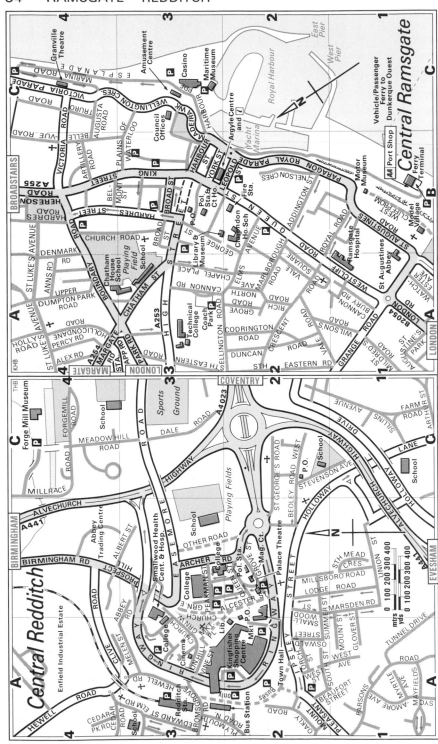

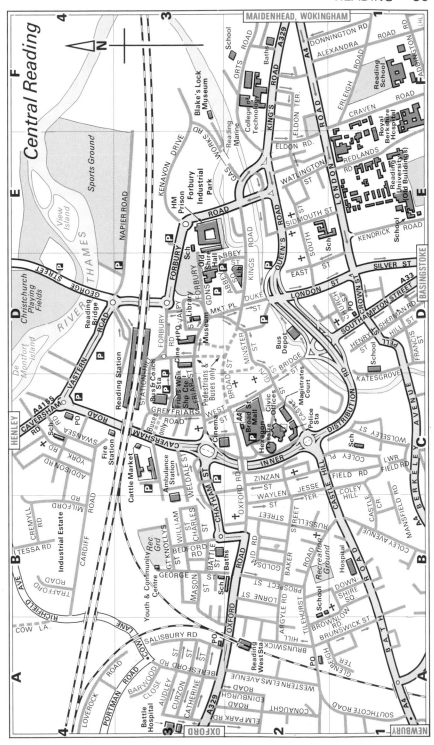

Central Reading

REIGATE

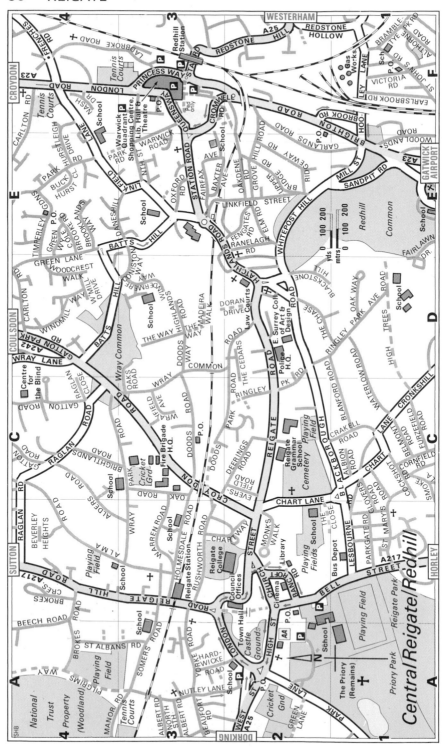

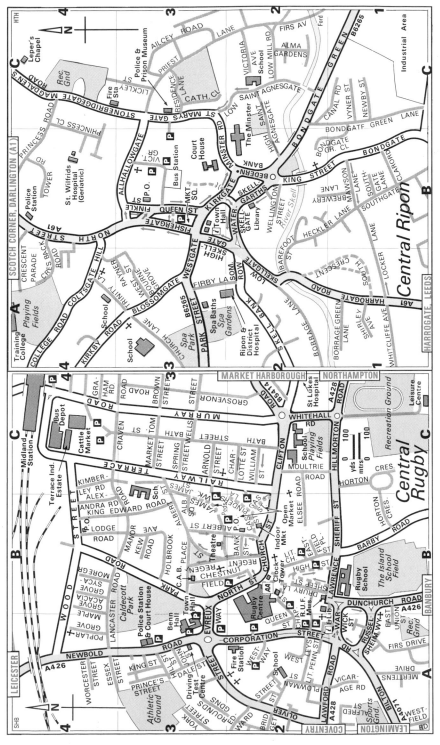

RUGBY RIPON

Central Ripon

HARROGATE, LEEDS

SCOTCH CORNER, DARLINGTON (A1)

Leper's Chapel
Rec Gnd
Police & Prison Museum
Fire Sta
CATH. CL.
The Minster
St. Wilfrids Hospital (Geriatric)
Police Station
P.O.
Court House
Bus Station
Town Hall
Library
Ripon & District Hospital
Spa Baths
Spa Gardens
School
Training College
Playing Fields

AILCEY ROAD
PRIEST LANE
RESIDENCE LANE
ST MARYS GATE
LICKLEY ST
STONEBRIDGEGATE
MAGDALEN'S ROAD
PRINCESS CL.
TOWER RD
NORTH STREET
CRESCENT PARADE
CRES BACK ROAD
COLLEGE ROAD
COLTSGATE HILL
KIRKBY ROAD
CHURCH LANE
PARK STREET
BLOSSOMGATE
TRINITY LA
WEST MOUNT
RAVNER
ALLHALLOWGATE
VICT. GR.
FINKLE ST
QUEEN ST
FISHERGATE
KIRKGATE
WESTGATE
HIGH SKELL
FIRBY LA
SKELL BANK ROW
LOW SKELLGATE
WATER SKELLGATE
SKELL GATE
GARITHS
SKELL
BANK
BEDERN
KING STREET
MINSTER RD
VICTORIA AVE
ALMA GARDENS
LOW MILL RD
FIRS AV
SAINT AGNESGATE
HIGH AGNESGATE
WELLINGTON STREET
BONDGATE
BONDGATE GREEN LANE
CANAL RD
VYNER ST
NEWBY ST
BONDGATE GR. CL.
MAWSON LANE
SOUTHGATE LANE
BREWERY
CLAROROAD
SOUTH GATE LANE
HECKLER LANE
BARFOOT LANE
BARROGATE ROAD
SOUTH CRESCENT
LOCKER
BORRAGE LANE
BORRAGE GREEN LANE
SHIRLEY AVE
WHIT CLIFFE AVE
River Skell
Ford
B6265
BONDGATE GREEN

Central Rugby

LEICESTER
MARKET HARBOROUGH
NORTHAMPTON
BANBURY
LEAMINGTON
COVENTRY

Midland Station
Bus Depot
Cattle Market
Terrace Ind. Estate
P.O.
Recreation Ground
St Lukes Hospital
Leisure Centre
School Playing Fields
School
Theatre
Clock Tower
Indoor Mkt
Open Mkt
C.A.B. Place
Caldecott Park
Police Station & Court House
Benn Hall
Town Hall
Rugby Centre
R.U.F. Mus.
Rugby School
The Island School Field
Fire Station
Test Centre
Driving Centre
Athletic Ground
Sports Gnd.

GRAHAM RD
BROWN ROAD
GROSVENOR ROAD
MURRAY ROAD
CRAVEN ST
MARKET ST
TOM STREET
BATH STREET
SPRING STREET
WELLS STREET
ARNOLD STREET
CHAR. ST
LOTTE ST
WILLIAM ST
CLIFTON RD
HILLMORTON ROAD
MOULTRIE ROAD
HORTON CRES.
WHITEHALL RD
TERRACE
RAILWAY
KIMBERLEY RD
ALEX-ANDRA RD
KING EDWARD ROAD
JAMES ST
ALBERT ST
ALB. SQ.
PINDERS
ELSEE ROAD
CHURCH ST
SHERIFF ST
BARBY ROAD
HORTON CRES.
FIELD
MANOR ROAD
KEW AVE
HOLBROOK AVE
REGENT ST
CHESTNUT FIELD
NORTH ST
QUEEN ST
HIGH ST
DRURY LA
LAWRENCE ST
DUNCHURCH ROAD
EAST UNION ST
LIT. ELBOROW ST
EAST ST
FIELD
LODGE ROAD
P.O.
WOOD STREET
MOREGR ROAD
LANCASTER ROAD
PARK ROAD
EVREUX WAY
NEWBOLD ROAD
WORCESTER STREET
ESSEX STREET
KING ST
PRINCE'S STREET
YORK STREET
HILL ST
DALES PL
GROUNDS GDNS
OLIVER ST
WARD ST
BRIDGET ST
GET ST
PLOWMAN ST
LIT. PENN. ST
WEST ST
WEST. WAY
LAWFORD ROAD
VICARAGE RD
WICK ST
RUSSELL ST
SHEIM WY
FIRS DRIVE
MARTENS DRIVE
BILTON RD
WEST-FIELD
ALFRED ST
GROVE
SYCA-MORE GROVE
ACACIA GROVE
MAPLE GROVE
POPLAR
A426
A428
A4
A071
A426
B5414

POPLAR

yds 0 100
mtrs 0 100

SHB
HTH

ROCHDALE

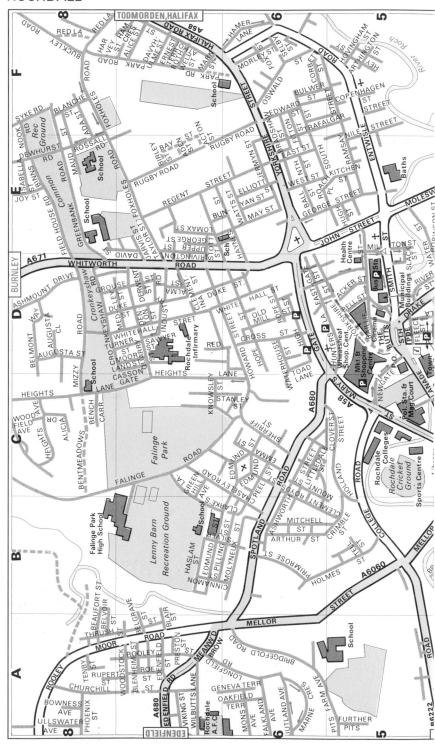

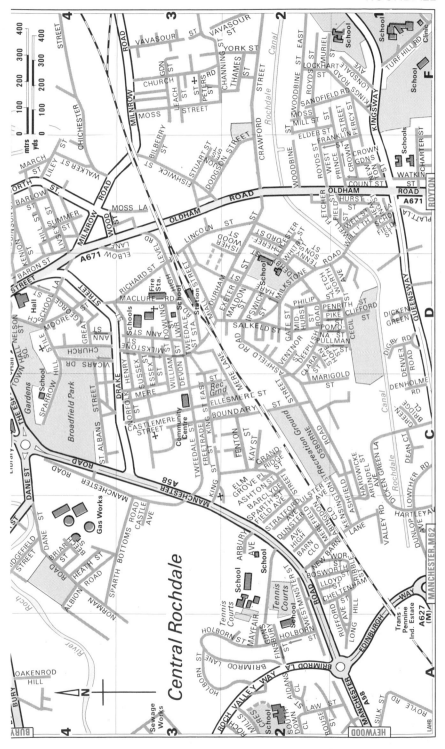

Central Rochdale

ST ANDREWS

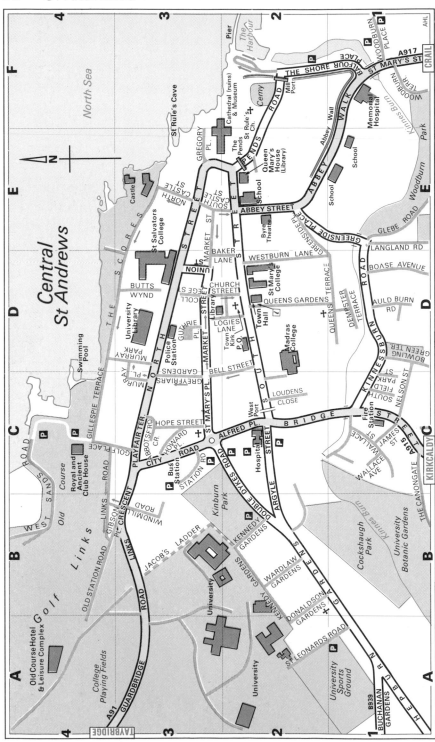

Central St Andrews

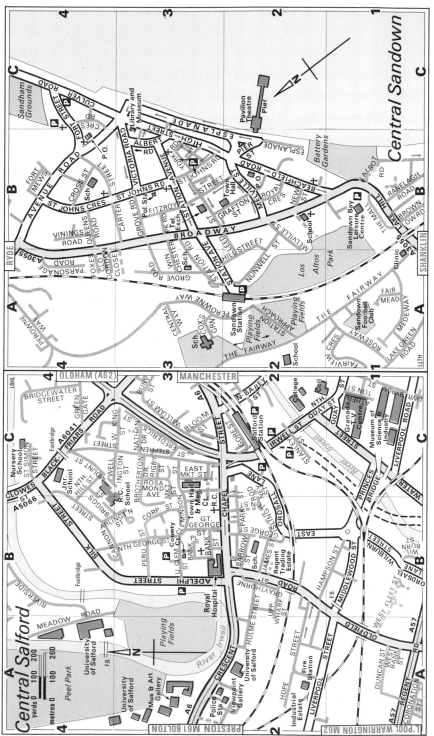

SALFORD SANDOWN

Central Sandown

Central Salford

SALISBURY

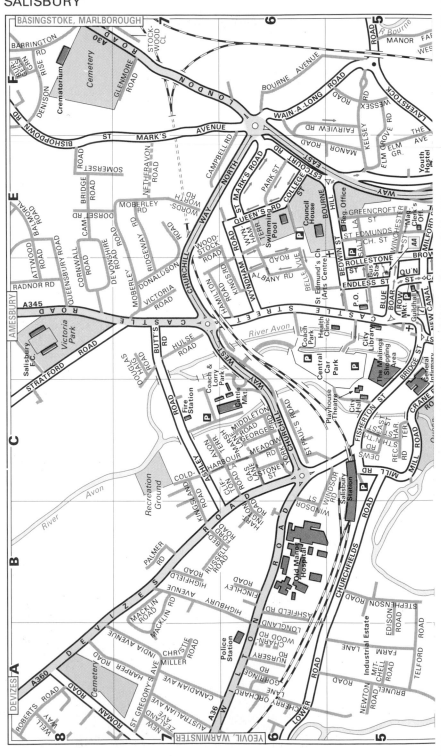

SALISBURY

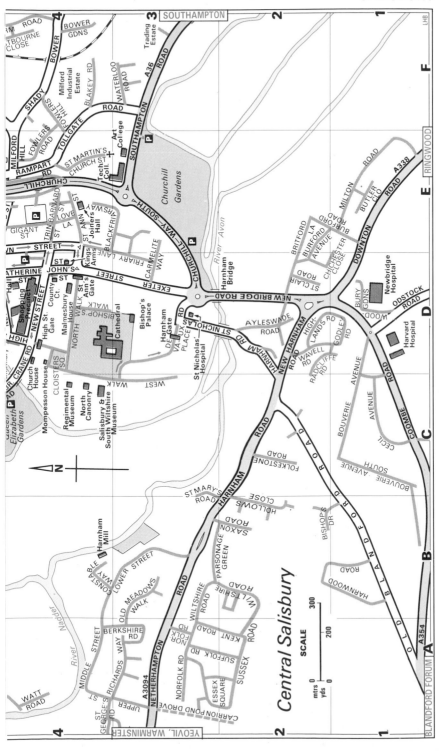

Central Salisbury

SHEFFIELD

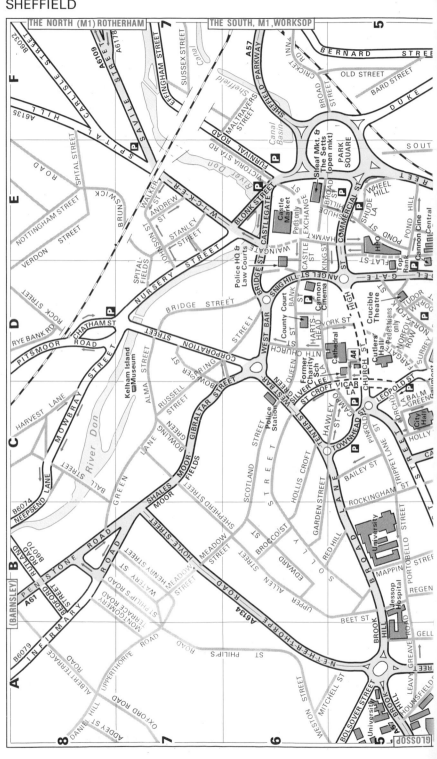

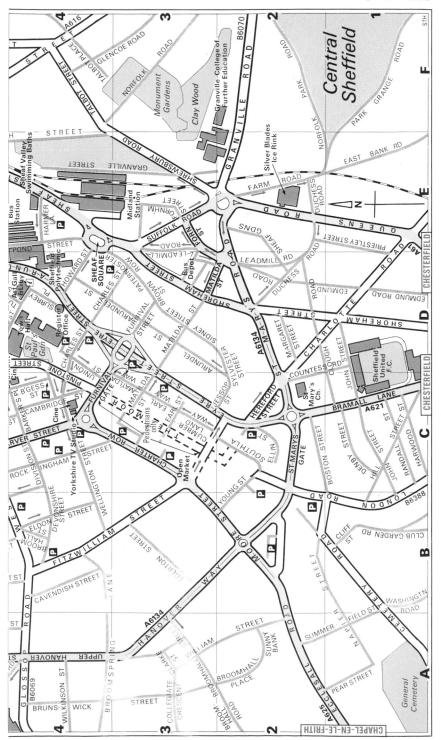

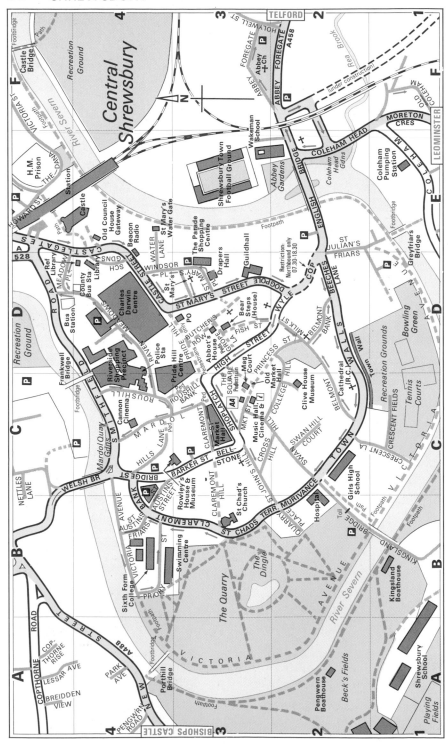

SHREWSBURY

Central Shrewsbury

SLOUGH

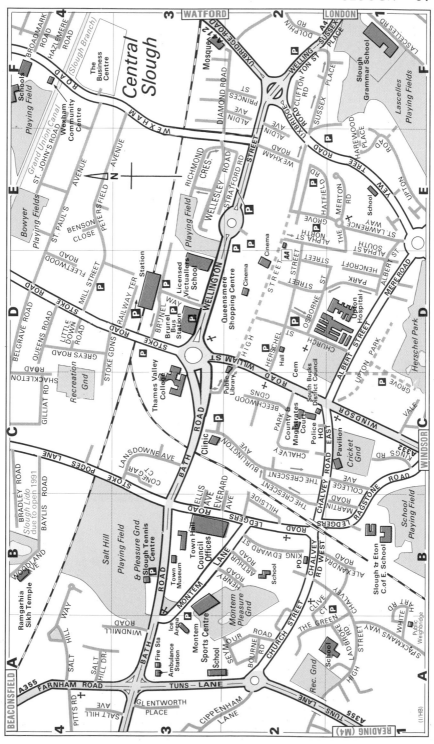

SOUTHAMPTON

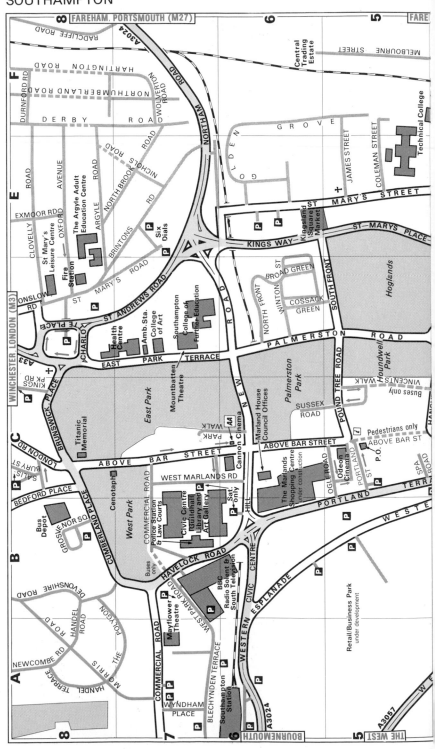

SOUTHAMPTON

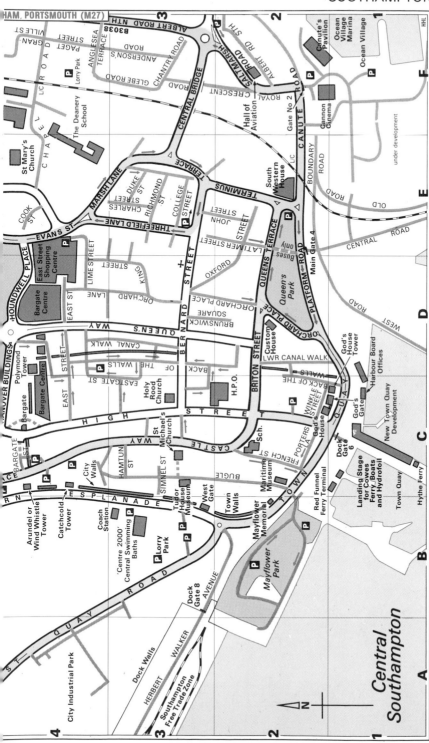

Central Southampton

STOKE STOCKTON

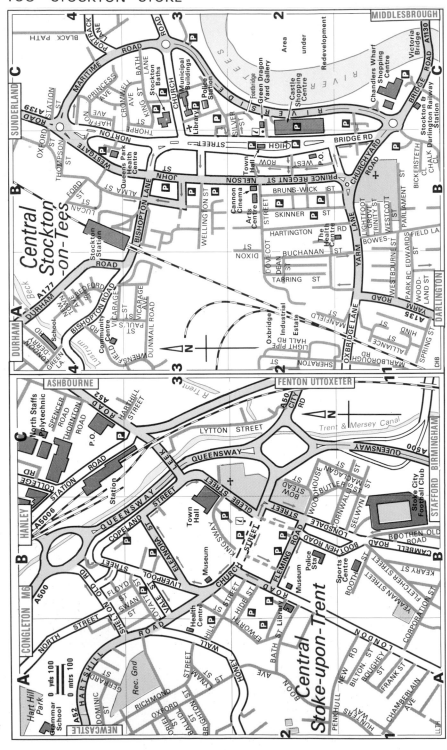

STOCKTON

Central Stockton-on-Tees

MIDDLESBROUGH

RIVER TEES

Area under Redevelopment

Victoria Bridge

Chandlers Wharf Shopping Centre

Green Dragon Yard Gallery

Castle Shopping Centre

Footbridge

Stockton & Darlington Railway Station

CHALK

BICKERSTETH CL

PARLIAMENT

Municipal Buildings

Stockton Baths

Police Station

Library

Town Hall

P.O.

HIGH STREET

WEST ROW

BRIDGE RD

CHURCHYARD ROAD

BRIDGE RD

BRIDGE RD

Queens Park Health Centre

PRINCE REGENT ST

NELSON STREET

BRUNS-WICK ST

SKINNER ST

The Health Centre

YARM RD

HARTINGTON ST

BUCHANAN ST

DEAN ST

TARRING ST

DIXON ST

DOVECOT ST

WELLINGTON ST

Cannon Cinema

Arts Centre

JOHN ST

BISHOPTON LANE

ALMA ST

LUCAN ST

Stockton Station

MARITIME

PORTRACK LANE

BLACK PATH

BATH LANE

KING ST

SILVER ST

CHURCH ROAD

PRINCESS AVE

CROMWELL AVE

STOCKTON AVE

THORPE ST

HARTBURN AVE

NORTON RD

WESTGATE

THOMPSON ST

OXFORD RD

SUNDERLAND ROAD A139

BEDFORD ST

NEWTON ST

DURHAM RD A177

Beck

VICARAGE RD

ST PAUL'S RD

DUNMAIL ROAD

WHENSFIELD ROAD

Lustrum

Community Centre

School

GREEN LANE

LONDON DERRY RD

Oxbridge Industrial Estate

MANFIELD ST

LIGHT PIPE HALL RD

SHERATON ST

OXBRIDGE LANE

MARLBOROUGH RD

ALLIANCE ST

HIND ST

SPRING ST

CHB

YARM LANE

YARM ROAD A135

DARLINGTON

WOOD-LAND ST

PARK RD

EDWARDS ST

WESTBOURNE ST

BOWES RD

LIGHTFOOT GROVE

TRINITY ST

WESTCOTT ST

FIELD LA

STOKE

Central Stoke-upon-Trent

ASHBOURNE

North Staffs Polytechnic

P.O.

HARTHILL STREET

LYTTON STREET

QUEENSWAY

Station

Town Hall

Museum

Health Centre

Museum

Police Sta

Sports Centre

Stoke City Football Club

FENTON UTTOXETER

Trent & Mersey Canal

CITY RD

A50

QUEENSWAY A500

BOW STEAD ST

WOODHOUSE ST

BUTLER ST

CORNWALL ST

SELWYN ST

MALAGAN ST

LONSDALE ST

BOOTHEN OLD ROAD

CAMPBELL ROAD

KEARY ST

YEAMAN STREET

FLETCHER STREET

BOOTHEN RD

GLEBE STREET

FLEMING ROAD

HIDE ST

EPWORTH ST

CHURCH STREET

KINGSWAY

LIVERPOOL STREET

ELEANORA STREET

COPELAND ST

WYATT ST

SHELTON OLD ROAD

FLOYD ST

SWAN ST

VALE ST

BATH ST

Library

HILL ST

HONEYWALL

London RD

HUNTERS WAY

PENKHULL NEW RD

BOUGHEY RD

BILTON ST

FRANK ST

CHAMBERLAIN AVE

CORPORATION ST

LONDON ROAD

BIRMINGHAM A500

STAFFORD

HANLEY

STATION RD

COLLEGE RD

SPENCER ROAD

THORNTON ROAD

A52 ROAD

CONGLETON M6

NORTH STREET

A500

HARTSHILL ROAD

GERRARD ST

NYNAM ST

RICHMOND ST

OXFORD ST

ORIEL ST

BAYLTON ST

BRISTON ST

DOMINIC ST

A52 NEWCASTLE

Rec. Grd

Hart Hill Park

Grammar School

0 yds 100

0 mtrs 100

STRATFORD SWANAGE

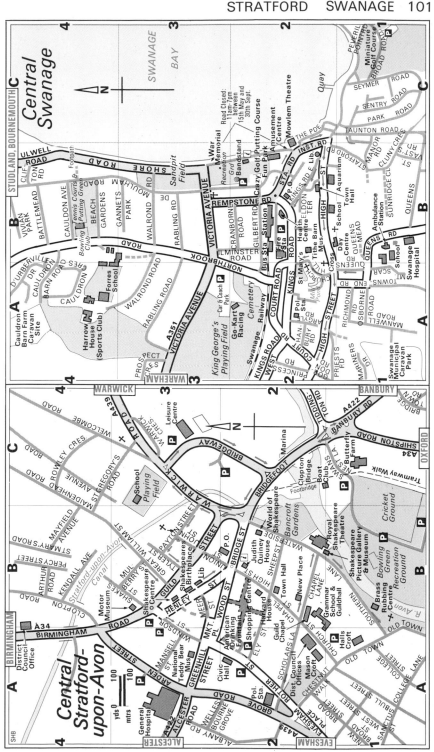

Central Swanage

Road Closed: 11am-7pm between 15th May and 30th Sept.

STUDLAND, BOURNEMOUTH

SWANAGE BAY

War Memorial
Bandstand
Recreation Grd
Amusement Centre
Mowlem Theatre
Quay
THE PDE
Fun Park
Crazy Golf Putting Course
Peveril Point
Miniature Golf Course
BROAD ROAD
SEYMER ROAD
SENTRY ROAD
PARK ROAD
MANOR ROAD
TAUNTON ROAD
CLUNY CRES
SUNRIDGE CL
QUEENS ST
VAST ST

ULWELL ROAD
SHORE ROAD
MOULHAM ROAD
Sandpit Field
Footpath
Tennis Courts
Putting Green
Bowling Club
BEACH GARDENS
GANNETS PARK
WALROND PARK
DE RABLING RD
VICTORIA AVENUE
CRANBORNE
REMPSTONE RD
ILMINSTER ROAD
NORTHBROOK ROAD
GILBERT RD
STA. RD
Bus Sta
Fire Sta
Railway Station
P.O.
KINGS RD E. Lib
STAFFORD RD
HIGH ST
ELDON TER
Aquarium
Town Hall
School
Day Centre
St Mary's Health Centre
Tithe Barn Mus
CHURCH Cross
MEAD
Ambulance Station
QUEENS RD
SCAR MT
School
Swanage Hospital

CLIFTON RD
VIVIAN PARK
BATTLEMEAD
CAULDON AVE
D'URBERVILLE DR
CAULDRON CRES
BARN ROAD
CAULDRON ROAD
Forres School
WALROND ROAD
RABLING ROAD
A251 VICTORIA AVENUE
PROSPECT CRES
Cauldron Barn Farm Caravan Site
Harrow House (Sports Club)
King George's Playing Field
Go-Kart Racing
Car & Coach Park
Swanage Cemetery
COURT ROAD
KINGS ROAD
WEST ST
PRINCES RD
HAN. RD
BURY RD
Pol. Sta
HIGH STREET
CHURCH RD
QUEENS RD
TOWNS END RD
RICHMOND RD
OSBORNE RD
PRIESTS RD
MARINERS DR
MANWELL ROAD
GR
Swanage Municipal Caravan Park

WARWICK

Central Stratford-upon-Avon

BIRMINGHAM
A34
CLOPTON ROAD
MAIDENHEAD ROAD
ROWLEY CRES
WELCOMBE ROAD
WARWICK ROAD A439
ST GREGORY'S ROAD
School Playing Field
Leisure Centre
BRIDGEWAY
Marina
Clopton Bridge
Boat Club
Footbridge
BANBURY
A422 BANBURY RD
A34
SHIPSTON ROAD
OXFORD
BRIDGE TOWN RD
Butterfly Farm
Tramway Walk
Cricket Ground
TIDDINGTON RD
SWANS NEST LA

District Council Office
Motor Museum
Shakespeare's Centre
Shakespeare's Birthplace
Lib
GUILD ST
HENLEY ST
BRIDGE ST
World of Shakespeare
Bancroft Gardens
Judith Quiney House
Town Hall
New Place
Royal Shakespeare Theatre
Shakespeare Picture Gallery & Museum
Bowling Green
Recreation Ground
Brass Rubbing Centre
OLD TOWN
R. Avon

MAYFIELD AVENUE
ST MARY'S ROAD
ARTHUR ROAD
PERCY STREET
KENDALL AVE
Stratford-upon-Avon Canal
SHAKESPEARE ST
GREAT WILLIAM ST
PAYTON STREET
TYLER ST
SHN
MULBERRY ST
WINDSOR ST
MEER ST
WOOD ST
UNION ST
HIGH ST
SHEEP ST
CHAPEL ST
WATERSIDE
SOUTHERN LANE
CHAPEL LANE
Grammar School & Guildhall
Halls Croft
National Teddy Bear Mus
American Drinking Fountain
Shopping Centre
Civic Hall
Guild Chapel
Mason Croft
Dist. Council Offices
Pol. Sta
General Hospital
ARDEN STREET
MANSELL ST
GREENHILL ST
MKT. PL.
ELY ST
SCHOLARS LA
ROTHER ST
CHURCH ST
CHESTNUT WALK
OLD TOWN
GROVE ROAD
WELLESBOURNE GROVE
BROAD WALK
ALBANY RD
BIRMINGHAM ROAD
ALCESTER ROAD
A422
A439
EVESHAM
ALCESTER
BROAD ST
WEST STREET
SANCTUS STREET
NEW BROAD STREET
SHAKESPEARE ST
SANCTUS ROAD
COLLEGE LANE
COLLEGE STREET
TRINBULL STREET
BRIDGE TOWN RD

yds 0   100
mtrs 0   100

N

SHB

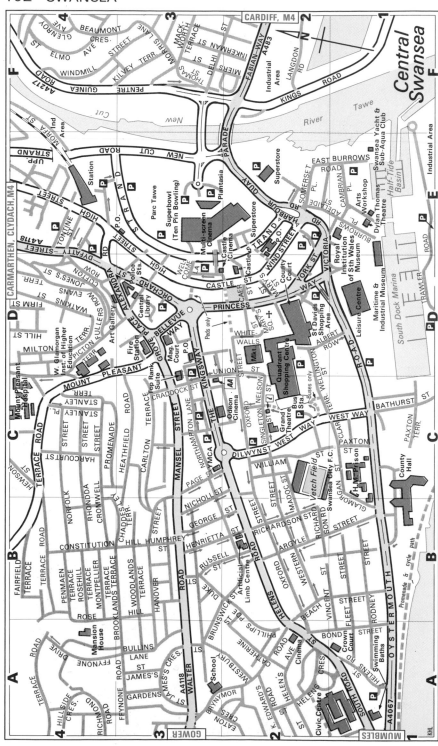

SWINDON

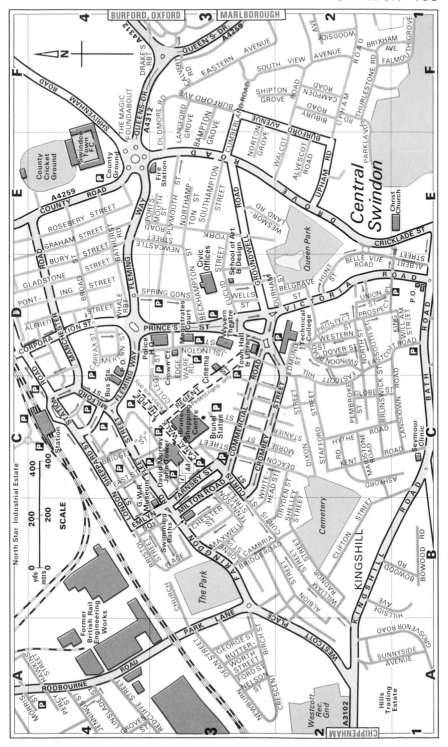

WARWICK   WINDSOR

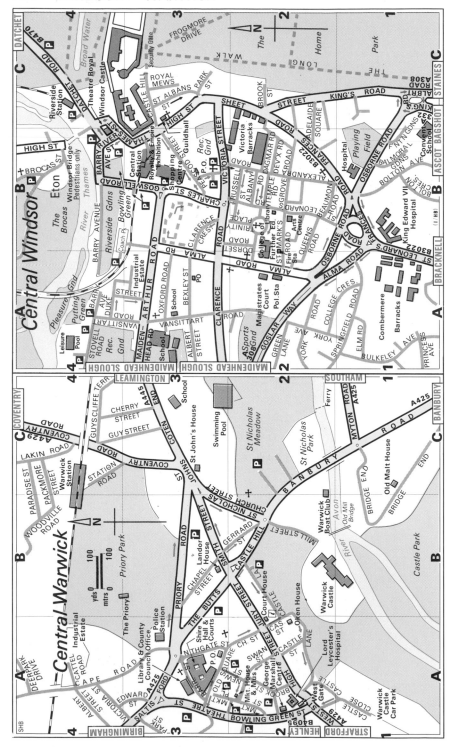

WINDSOR

DATCHET

Broad Water

B470

ROAD

Theatre Royal

Windsor Castle

ROYAL MEWS

ST ALBANS

Riverside Station

FROGMORE DRIVE

Security Gate

THE WALK

LONG

The Home Park

N

3   2   1

C

A308 STAINES

ASCOT BAGSHOT

HIGH ST

BROCAS

Eton

The Brocas

River Thames

Windsor Bridge
Pedestrians only

Riverside Gdns

Bowling Green

Coach Pk

BARRY AVENUE

DATCHET

MEWS

CASTLE HILL

HIGH ST

ST

ST ALBANS ST

SHEET ST

BROOK ST

KING'S ROAD

Central Station

Royalty & Empire Exhibition

Shopping Centre

Guildhall

P.O. Gnd

VICTORIA STREET

Victoria Barracks

DAGMAR RD

DEVX RD

ADELAIDE SQUARE

KING'S ROAD

Hospital

Playing Field

OSBORNE ROAD

FNTN GDNS

BALMORAL GDNS

BOLTON AVE

Convent School

B3022

B

BRACKNELL

Central Windsor

The Brocas

BARRY AVENUE

GOSWELL ROAD

CHARLES ST

Rec. Gnd

RUSSELL ST

ALBANY

TEMPLE

SGROVE RD

ST LEONARD'S

College of Further Ed

Library

Arts Centre

ST MARK'S

QUEENS ROAD

BEAUMONT ST

Fire Station

FIRE ROAD

OSBORNE ROAD

B3022

ST LEONARD'S ROAD

BRANCES RD

King Edward VII Hospital

(I/HB)

A

Pleasure Gnd

Putting Gnd

BARRY AVE

DUKE ST

STREET

STOVELL ROAD

MAIDENHEAD RD

Industrial Estate

ARTHUR ROAD

OXFORD ROAD

BEXLEY ST

School

PO

VANSITTART

ALBERT STREET

CLARENCE CRES

CLARENCE ROAD

ALMA RD

ALMA ROAD

Magistrates Court

Pol. Sta

DORSET ROAD

GOSLAR WAY

Sports Gnd

GREEN LANE

York Ave

COLLEGE CRES

ALMA ROAD

Combermere Barracks

SPRINGFIELD ROAD

ELM RD

BULKELEY AVE

PRINCESS AVE

Leisure Pool

P Rec. Gnd

School

A Sports 30 Gnd

C   4   3   2   1

LEAMINGTON

MAIDENHEAD SLOUGH

SOUTHAM

WARWICK

COVENTRY

A429 ROAD

LAKIN ROAD

PARADISE ST

PACKMORE STREET

WOODVILLE ROAD

Warwick Station

STATION ROAD

GUYS CLIFFE TERR

CHERRY STREET

GUY STREET

COTEN END

A445

LEAMINGTON

COVENTRY ROAD

JOHNS ST

St John's House

PRIORY ROAD

Priory Park

School

Swimming Pool

St Nicholas Meadow

ST NICHOLAS STREET

CHURCH STREET

St Nicholas Park

Ferry

MYTON ROAD

A425

BANBURY ROAD

A425

BANBURY

C

Old Malt House

Avon

Old Mill Bridge

Warwick Boat Club

BRIDGE END

BRIDGE END

B

Central Warwick

N

100   0   100
yds   0
mtrs

The Priory

CATTEL ROAD

Industrial Estate

DEER PARK DRIVE

Police Station

Library & County Council Office

Landor House

Chapel Street

SMITH STREET

GERRARD ST

CASTLE HILL

THE BUTTS

Court House

Oken House

Warwick Castle

Castle Park

River

Castle Park

A

Shire Hall & Courts

NITHGATE ST

SQUARE

OLD SQUARE

P.O.

Marshall Centre

Mkt House & Mus

George

St MARY'S CH ST

SWAN ST

JURY STREET

HIGH ST

Oken House

CASTLE ST

CAS ST

CASTLE LANE

Lord Leycester's Hospital

Warwick Castle Car Park

VICTORIA STREET

ALBERT STREET

SALTIS FORD

EDWARD ST

CAPE ROAD

A425

PARK ST

THEATRE ST

BARRACK ST

BOWLING GREEN ST

NEW ST

WEST ST

A429

West Gate

CASTLE CLOSE

B4095

A   4   3   2   1

BIRMINGHAM   STRATFORD HENLEY   BANBURY

SHB

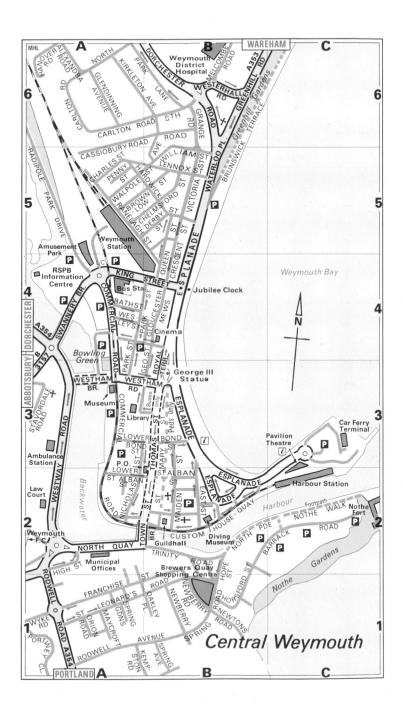

Central Weymouth

WEMBLEY

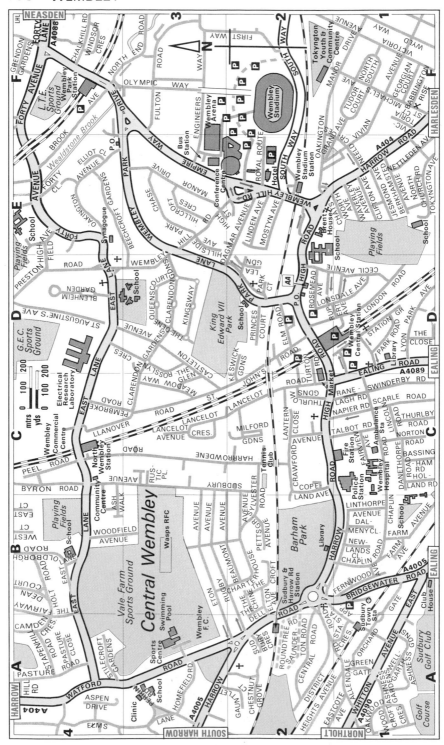

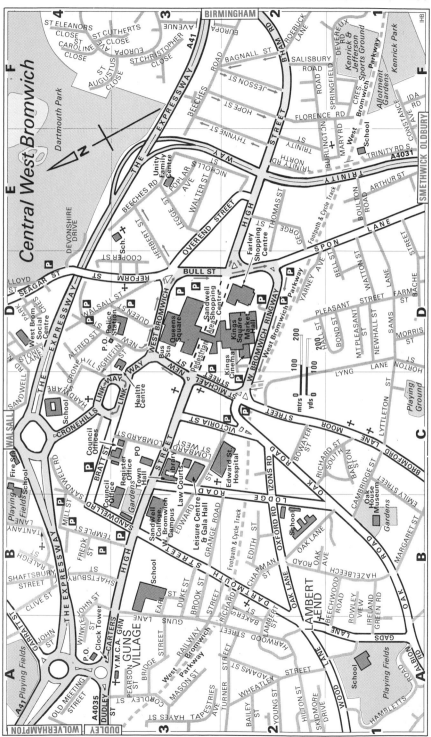

WEST BROMWICH

WINCHESTER

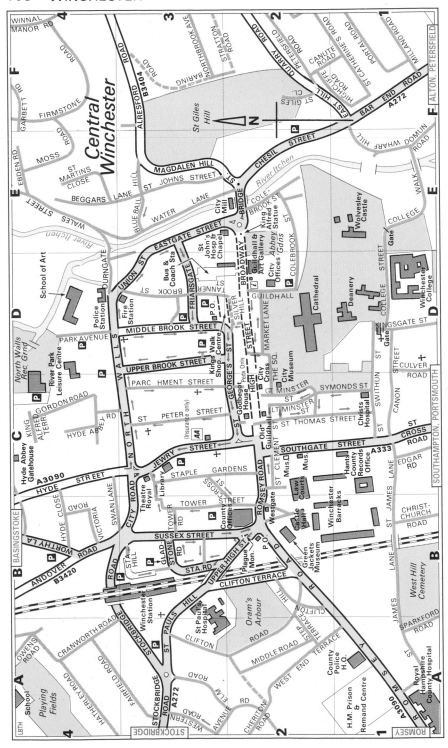

Central Winchester

WOKING

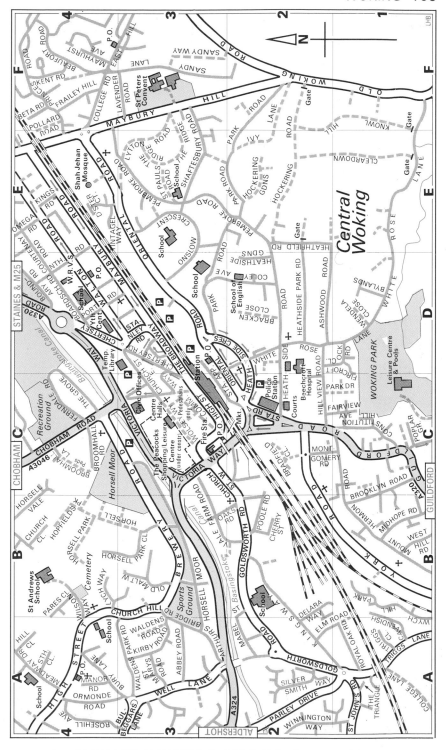

Central Woking

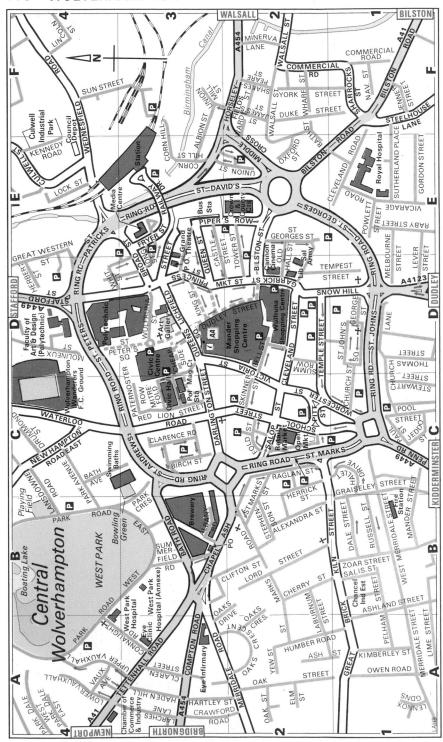

WORCESTER

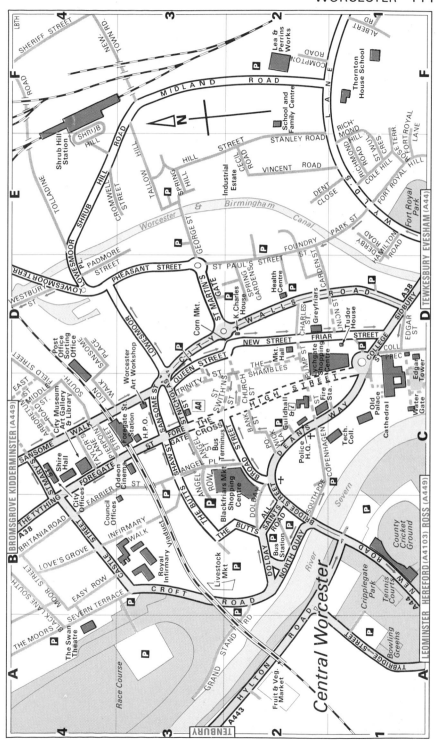

Central Worcester

YORK

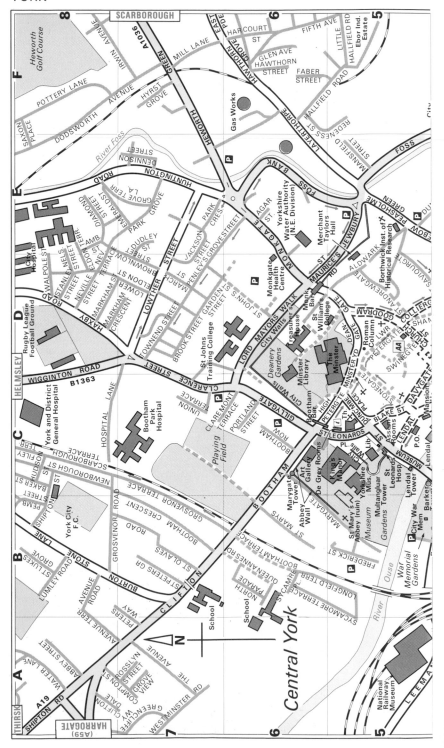

Central York

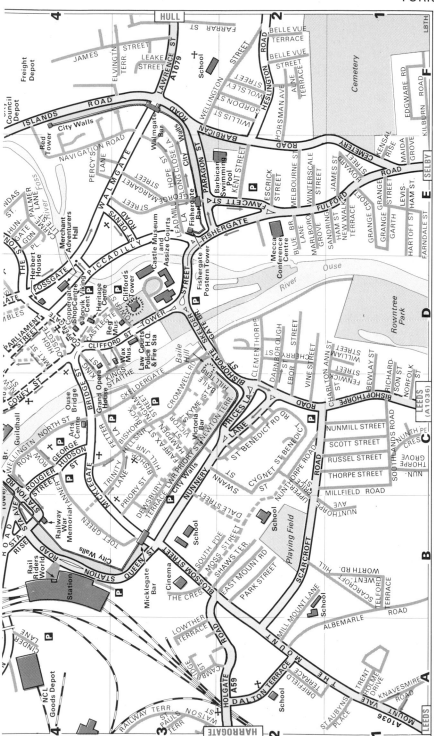

BIRMINGHAM AIRPORT

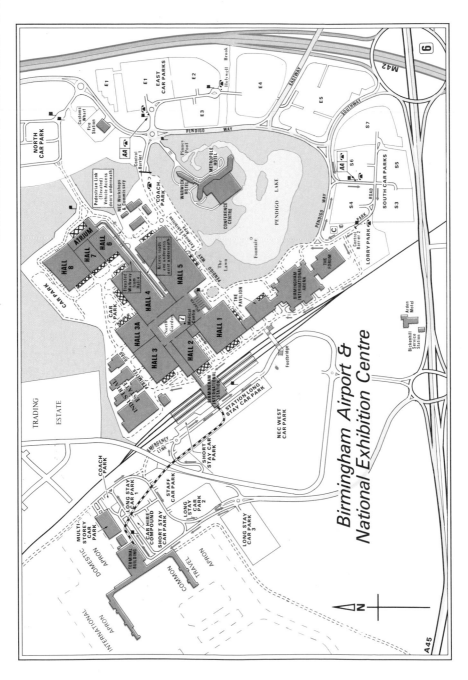

*Birmingham Airport &
National Exhibition Centre*

EDINBURGH AIRPORT

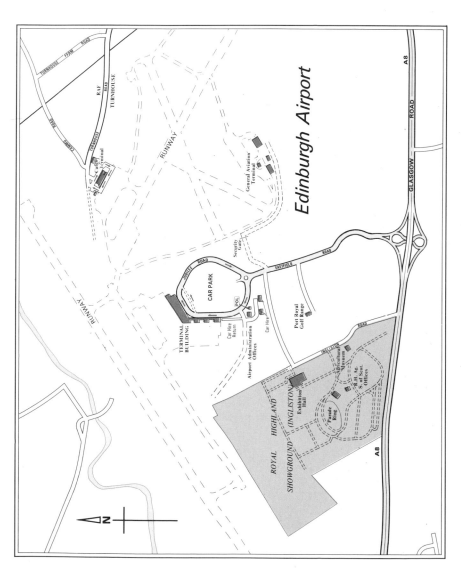

EAST MIDLANDS AIRPORT

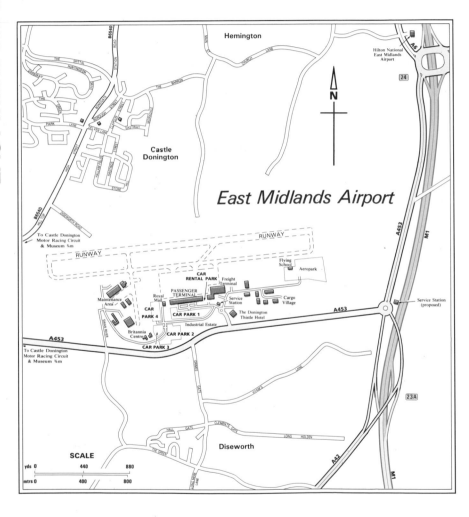

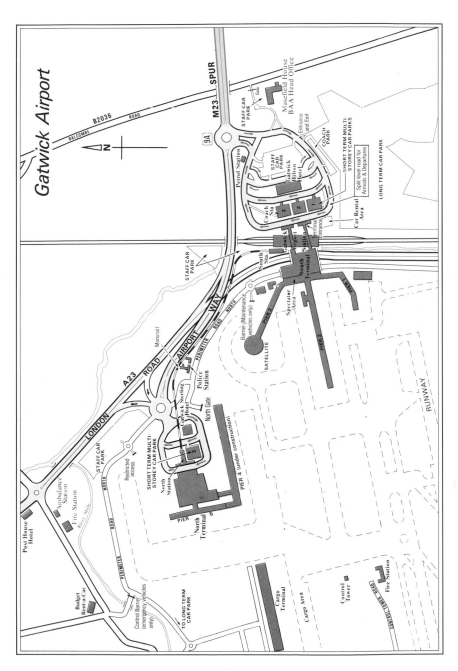

GATWICK AIRPORT

GLASGOW AIRPORT

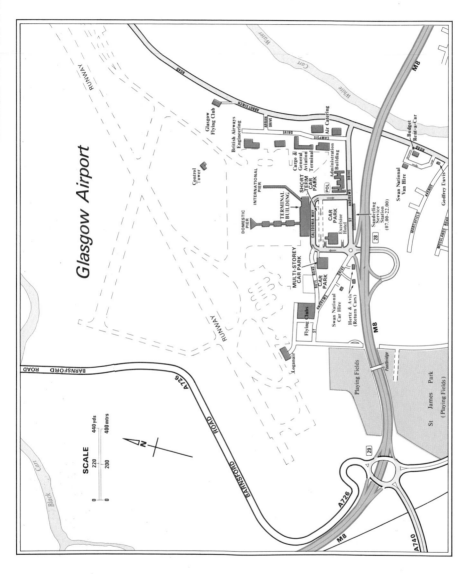

Glasgow Airport

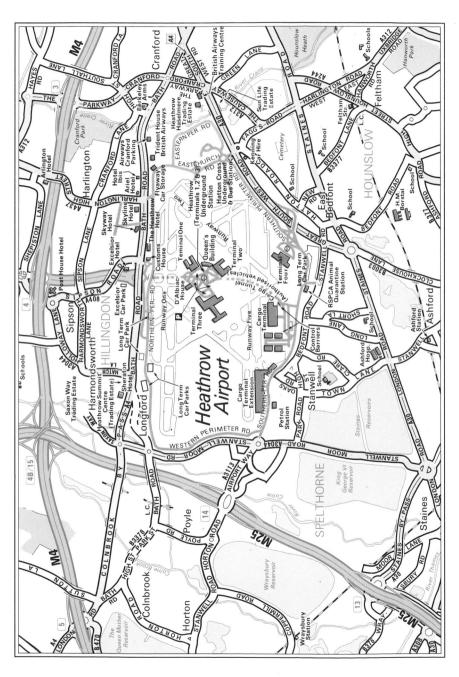

HEATHROW AIRPORT

LONDON CITY AIRPORT

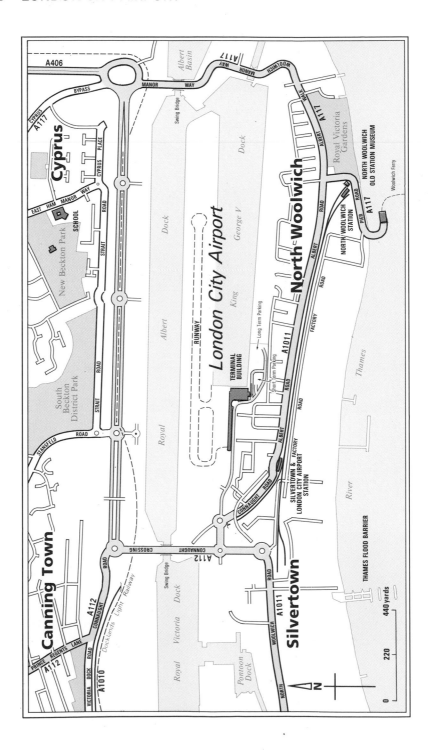

LUTON AIRPORT

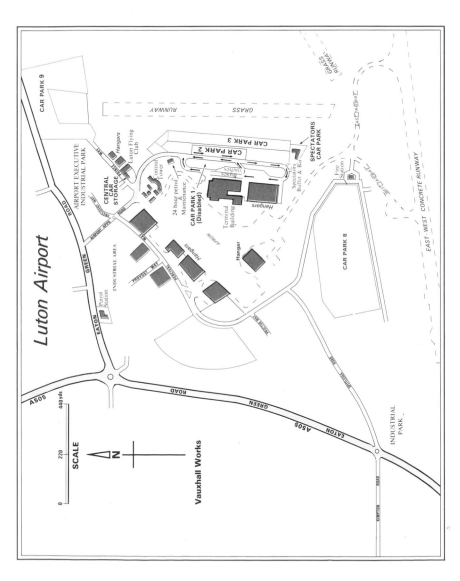

Luton Airport

MANCHESTER AIRPORT

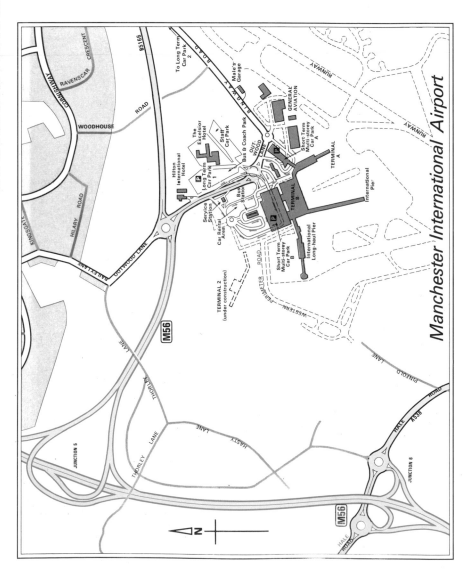

Manchester International Airport

To Long Term Car Park 2

Male's Garage

GENERAL AVIATION

Short Term Multi-storey Car Park A

The Excelsior Hotel

Staff Car Park

Bus & Coach Park

OUTWOOD LANE

TERMINAL A

Hilton International Hotel

Long Term Car Park 1

Bus Station

TERMINAL B

International Pier

Service Station

Car Rental Area

Short Term Multi-storey Car Park B

International Long-haul Pier

PERIMETER ROAD

WESTERN

TERMINAL 2
(under construction)

RUNWAY

RUNWAY

CORNISHWAY

RAVENSCAR CRESCENT

B5166

WOODHOUSE

ROAD

HILARY ROAD

KINGSGATE

RAILEY LANE

OUTWOOD LANE

M56

LANE

THORLEY LANE

THORLEY LANE

HASTY LANE

JUNCTION 5

PINFOLD LANE

HALE ROAD

A538

JUNCTION 6

M56

HALE ROAD

N

STANSTED AIRPORT

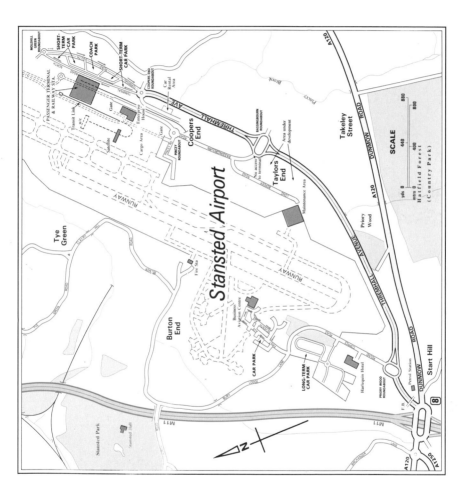

Distance Chart

The distances between towns on the mileage chart are given to the nearest mile, and are measured along the normal AA recommended routes. It should be noted that AA recommended routes do not necessarily follow the shortest distances between places but are based on the quickest travelling time, making maximum use of motorways or dual-carriageway roads.

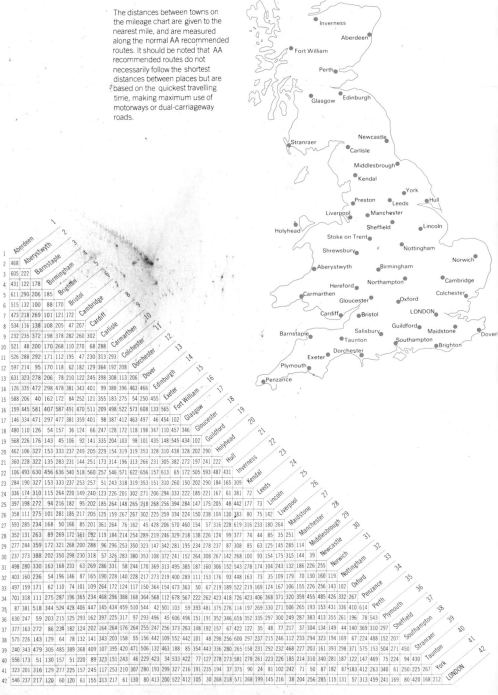

	1 Aberdeen	2 Aberystwyth	3 Barnstaple	4 Birmingham	5 Brighton	6 Bristol	7 Cambridge	8 Cardiff	9 Carlisle	10 Carmarthen	11 Colchester	12 Dorchester	13 Dover	14 Edinburgh	15 Exeter	16 Fort William	17 Glasgow	18 Gloucester	19 Guildford	20 Holyhead	21 Hull	22 Inverness	23 Kendal	24 Leeds	25 Lincoln	26 Liverpool	27 Maidstone	28 Manchester	29 Middlesbrough	30 Newcastle	31 Norwich	32 Nottingham	33 Oxford	34 Penzance	35 Perth	36 Plymouth	37 Sheffield	38 Southampton	39 Stranraer	40 Taunton	41 York
2	468																																								
3	605	222																																							
4	431	122	178																																						
5	611	290	206	185																																					
6	515	132	100	88	170																																				
7	473	218	269	101	121	172																																			
8	534	116	138	108	205	47	207																																		
9	232	235	372	198	378	282	260	302																																	
10	521	48	200	170	268	110	270	68	288																																
11	526	288	292	171	112	195	47	230	313	293																															
12	597	214	95	170	118	62	182	129	364	192	208																														
13	631	323	278	206	78	210	122	245	398	308	113	206																													
14	126	335	472	298	478	381	343	401	99	388	396	463	466																												
15	588	206	40	162	172	84	252	121	355	183	275	54	250	455																											
16	159	445	581	407	587	491	470	511	209	498	522	573	608	133	565																										
17	146	334	471	297	477	381	359	401	98	387	412	463	497	46	454	102																									
18	480	110	126	54	157	36	124	66	247	128	172	118	198	347	110	457	346																								
19	568	226	176	143	45	106	92	141	335	204	103	98	101	435	148	545	434	102																							
20	462	106	327	153	333	237	249	205	229	154	319	353	328	310	438	328	202	290																							
21	360	228	322	135	283	231	144	251	173	314	196	313	266	231	305	382	272	197	241	222																					
22	106	493	630	456	636	540	518	560	257	546	571	622	656	157	613	65	172	505	593	487	431																				
23	284	190	327	153	333	237	253	257	51	243	318	319	353	51	310	260	150	202	290	184	165	309																			
24	336	174	310	115	264	220	149	240	123	226	201	302	271	206	294	333	222	185	221	167	61	381	72																		
25	397	198	272	94	216	182	95	202	185	264	148	265	218	268	256	394	284	147	175	205	48	442	177	73																	
26	358	111	275	101	281	185	217	205	125	159	267	267	302	225	259	334	224	150	238	104	130	383	80	75	142																
27	593	285	234	168	50	166	85	201	361	264	76	162	45	428	206	570	460	154	57	316	228	619	316	233	180	264															
28	352	131	263	89	269	172	161	192	119	184	214	254	289	219	246	329	218	138	226	124	99	377	74	44	51	35	251														
29	277	244	359	172	321	268	200	288	96	296	253	350	323	147	342	281	195	234	278	237	87	308	85	63	125	145	285	114													
30	237	273	388	202	350	298	230	318	57	326	283	380	353	108	372	241	152	264	308	267	142	268	100	93	154	175	315	144	39												
31	498	280	300	163	168	231	63	269	286	331	58	244	170	369	313	495	385	187	160	306	152	543	278	174	104	243	132	186	226	255											
32	403	160	236	54	196	146	87	165	190	228	140	228	217	273	219	400	289	111	153	176	93	448	163	73	35	109	179	70	130	160	119										
33	497	159	171	62	110	74	101	109	264	172	124	117	150	364	154	473	363	50	67	219	189	522	219	169	124	167	106	155	226	256	143	102									
34	701	318	111	275	287	196	365	234	468	296	388	168	364	568	112	678	567	222	262	423	418	726	423	406	368	371	320	359	455	485	426	332	267								
35	87	381	518	344	524	428	406	447	145	434	459	510	544	42	501	103	59	393	481	375	276	114	197	269	330	271	506	265	193	153	431	336	410	614							
36	630	247	59	203	215	125	293	162	397	225	317	97	293	496	45	606	496	151	191	352	346	655	352	335	297	300	249	287	383	413	355	261	196	78	543						
37	377	163	272	86	231	182	124	202	164	264	176	264	255	247	256	373	263	148	192	157	67	422	122	35	48	77	217	37	104	134	149	44	140	369	310	297					
38	575	226	143	129	64	78	132	141	343	203	158	55	156	442	109	552	442	101	48	298	256	600	297	237	215	246	112	233	294	323	194	169	67	224	488	152	207				
39	240	343	479	305	485	389	409	107	395	420	471	506	132	463	188	85	354	483	226	487	203	161	393	298	371	575	153	504	271	450											
40	556	173	51	130	157	51	220	89	323	151	243	46	229	423	34	533	422	77	127	278	273	581	278	261	223	226	185	214	310	340	281	187	122	147	469	75	224	94	430		
41	323	201	316	129	277	225	157	245	117	253	210	307	280	193	299	327	216	191	235	194	37	375	90	24	81	102	242	71	50	87	182	87	183	412	263	340	61	250	225	267	
42	546	237	217	120	60	120	61	155	313	217	61	130	80	413	200	522	412	105	30	268	218	571	268	199	146	216	38	204	256	285	115	131	57	313	459	241	169	80	420	168	212